Iron Will

Iron Will

What one man needed to survive the blessing and the curse of the NFL

JAY FOREMAN

ISBN-13: 9780692878590
ISBN: 0692878599
Library of Congress Control Number: 2017905861
Foreman Books, Lincoln, NE

Dedications

To Soleil and Ciel, my two champions and heartbeats - with you my life is complete. You two are treasures from above.

To Francis Foreman, aka Papi, you are my hero.

To Joyce Garrison, you are my rock.

Finally, to my close friends and family, and especially my wife, your support and love is appreciated and will never be forgotten.

Chapters

Funny and real tidbits on a few subjects:
The Women-

I get asked all the time about what it is like as an athlete when it comes to the women. Obviously a lot of those questions come from assumptions and curiosity. I always laugh when people ask about it because in reality athletes are just like any other person walking the earth except we are more athletic a lot of the times.

The last part is that people look at athletes as dumb and all we do is play sports n fuck everything that moves. In some rare cases yes but what is the difference between athlete A or business person B? Nothing, except that athletes are higher profile and held to a higher standard.

The easiest way I can explain it to you is that as football players it's a little harder because of the physical and mental commitment you have to have in order to be good. Unlike other sports, we don't spend a lot of time in cities when we are on the road. We are on a schedule from the time we land until bed check and we leave right after the game is completed. I will say at the Super Bowl or pro Bowl there are a fair share of the same women(groupies) that are there and waiting but let's be honest most guys only go that route when it's their last choice. Plenty of women throw themselves at players and guys know where to go to find them when going out in their cities. It's as big or small as each individual makes it to be.

I can say without a doubt that I learned in college that there are girls that find themselves with or sleeping with numerous players over time. What's that mean? I don't know. LOL. I can say I have left girls once I found out they have slept with teammates or weren't upfront. Guys don't want to look like a fool unless it's on their own doing. I never judged I just adapted to the circumstances.

On a side note the funniest circumstance I ever personally encountered was when a prominent woman asked or proposed to me to sleep with her for an allowance. I couldn't hold back and laughed at first but this person was almost persuasive enough for me to consider. In the end I declined, have to have some pride right?

**** I will say the game has changed though. Back in the day the guys were the ones adding up women but now it's reversed. I have heard and met women that have "bagged" more athletes than they can count on their fingers and toes. What's that tell me? Athletes better keep their game and minds right cause these chicks are going for it all, your body and money. They have their own "hit list" like we used to.

The sad and funny part that have learned since returning to Nebraska is how silly and trifling grown men can be. We could be willing to give ourselves up for ne another on the field but as soon as they step off they trying to hate or throw salt on another man. Doesn't make sense. A wise man always said that a man's downfall is money, power and ponocho(google it). To this day I see cats tripping over themselves for chicks that are running game on them. The difference between male's n female's is that they will take it to their grave just to save face, us men make n announcement when we do something.

Teammates-

Throughout my whole career I can honestly say I have had only a handful on shitty teammates. What makes a teammate shitty? He has to do one or all of three things. Those three things would be that he's selfish, a snitch or mess with your money or home life. A selfish teammate is usually lazy, unreliable and only out for his personal gain. A teammate that is a snitch is the guy who is taking all the locker room talk upstairs to the powers that be. Every team has one or more and most of the time you don't find out until you are no longer on the team. These types of guys you can't trust but the worst part is that they usually last longer than you might. The last part is self-explanatory, some guys don't get it and will do anything out of jealousy. I will say that some of the best players in both college and NFL that I have met are the biggest let down. Why? Well because you expect them to have some sense of reality or something and some are just too caught up in themselve's and are assholes! The only way you will know is if you meet them face-to-face.

One

THE FOUNDATION

My grandpa always told me, *"Don't go knock at the door, kick it in and let them know you're in the building."* Little did I know how often I would have to reflect on that quote and the confidence it would give me to get by in the most trying times of my life.

I was born February 18, 1976 in Eden Prairie, Minnesota. My mom, Joyce Lewis-Garrison, was a flight attendant while my dad, Chuck Foreman, was a first-round draft pick in 1972 to the Minnesota Vikings. My parents were not married BUT somehow my dad had full custody. Since his schedule was so busy with football, I spent the majority of my childhood not living with him, but with my grandparents in Frederick, Maryland. During that time, I developed a huge respect for my grandparents, Janet and Francis Foreman. Most people assume my dad was my hero, rightfully so, but my hero was my grandfather and known to me as "Papi."

My grandfather had a military background and was a very prominent figure in the community. I was always allowed to run errands with him and he was constantly in my ear teaching me as much as he could about hard work and character. I loved asking him questions and listening to him talk. He held three jobs to make sure everyone in the family was taken care of, all while still attending to the "honey-do" lists my grandma would give him. He was a strong male figure in our family and set the standard high for me to always go above and beyond what was expected of me. In the summer, my cousin Craig would stay with us and we would go to "Crab-feast" in Frederick, Maryland. I loved it mainly because it was "all you could eat" and boy did I always put in work. This was where I fell in love with Maryland blue crabs. Maybe it was my young age or bias but I think Maryland blue crabs are second to none. Papi was a great cook and it seemed as though he would fry everything! I remember the cans of Crisco oil filled with grease to be used again for another meal. One thing we always did at their house was have family dinners. That is one thing I will never forget - the feeling of home.

My grandfather, Papi, the man who set the standard in our family. Even though he is gone, I still talk to him every day.

My grandma on the other hand was good at giving people chores to do. Funny thing is that I would grow to learn that she didn't discriminate on who she asked to do the chores. Her policy was if you are in her house you can work. At the time I hated it, but I surely miss those times as well.

One of my fondest memories from my time in Maryland was waiting with my cousin Craig for Grandma to come through that door. We'd look out the living room window and when we'd see her lights come around the corner we'd sprint down to the door.

At Christmas time, we would decorate the house and put reindeer figurines on the front lawn. Uncles, aunts, and friends would stop by during the holidays. There were always lots of stories being told and lots of food to eat. I learned so much just sitting there and listening to the adults talk. My family is very much an "alpha male" type of family. There are a lot of personalities, and typically they would all be in the kitchen arguing over the right and wrong ways to make the cornbread dressing. Papi would always tell me "the loudest person in the room is usually the weakest" and to "listen first and act second, be seen and not heard." I just watched and observed while trying to look busy when my grandma passed so she wouldn't find something for me to do. Papi had said that "great ones adjust," so by looking busy I had adjusted in a way that would get me out of house work.

My early childhood was filled with great memories, although I did miss my dad. He would come to visit but had to leave for football often. I remember crying in my room when he would leave for training camp. I didn't realize he was famous until I was older. He was so gracious to his fans. I wanted to play football just like him but he didn't want me to experience the pressure of following in his footsteps. Some of my warmest memories are of us watching football all day on Saturdays and Sundays. I now realize how much effort it took for my dad to do so, because like most retired players, he went through a time of when he absolutely hated football. I think football and the NFL make players feel like they gave so much and got so little in return when they hung up their cleats. I remember hearing my dad talk with former teammates and foes about the NFL, sometimes not with the fondest of memories. Little did I know that I would see their points in my own life but also grow to respect their view because of what they did to build the NFL to where it is today. Growing up with a famous father had its perks, but it also came with a lot of negative people who would have liked nothing else than to sit back and watch him, me, or both of us fail. I guess there were haters even back then. The good part about that was that it made us both go through it together, and it formed a bond that at times was unbreakable and special. He let me know I had to have higher standards in everything I did even when I thought it wasn't fair. I bet I heard "life isn't fair" about a million times. One thing it did was mature me in some areas faster than others, but it also held me back in other areas that affected me for a long time. I never wanted to put my dad in a position of overextending himself for my pleasure. Maybe that was an early sign that I would go on to do anything possible to get a college education for free.

My relationship with my mom as a child wasn't "normal" by the standards of the masses, but to me it was a foundation that helped me for a long time. I didn't grow up with my mom in the house day to day, but I knew she was with me every step of the way. One of my best memories of my mom wasn't even from her. I attended an elementary school called Forest Hills and I remember when my favorite teacher pulled me aside before recess and gave me cards my mom had sent to the school for me. I have never forgotten that because while my teacher read them to me she became emotional and cried and said, "You are one lucky young man." I looked forward to going to Arizona each summer to visit my mom. It was a yearly thing until I started to excel in sports. Even when my schedule became busy, I was able to see her a couple times a year when she would visit Minnesota. Even though she wasn't there physically I always felt like she was there for me.

My mom comes from a large, very intelligent, no nonsense family, but still fun. When I would visit her, she wasn't strict, but firm. She treated me like I was always living there, no special treatment. Another fond memory of my childhood was when I would go to the Boys and Girls club while she and my step-dad, Cliff, worked. I would play basketball every day. It was there that I started to grow as a child. Being from out of state and having to meet new kids and fit in was hard but taught me a lot. I was out of my comfort zone, but I soon met new friends and then began to know what it was like to compete.

My mom and I at my first birthday party. This picture is special because she always has had my back just like in this picture.

My time with my mom and Cliff wasn't the quantity that any of us wanted, but there sure were some quality times. My mom used to say, "We are making life long memories." She would always plan something fun for the end-of-year visit but I would have to earn it. She created a goal-oriented mindset for me at a very young age. Now as a man, I have the ultimate respect for her. She very well could have turned her back on me and washed her hands when she got the short end of the stick, but she didn't. I think some people like the idea of being a parent but don't like the responsibility. She definitely wasn't going to let circumstances stop her. I can remember getting a card she sent to my grandmother's house for me to read *every* Christmas. Little did I know I would find myself in a similar situation as an adult. She would always tell me before I would leave or get off the phone, "Jamal, keep doing right by yourself and other people and good things will always come your way, trust in God." At the time I rolled my eyes, but as an adult, I have realized just how true that is. Weird how my parents get smarter the older I get.

I remember we once drove from Phoenix to Las Vegas to go to Circus-Circus for our end-of-the-year festivity. I had never seen so many video games in my life! It was one of the happiest memories I had as a child and with her. I was very happy to have the structure of a mom and dad style life when I visited her and my step dad. The two households were a big contrast but were both helpful and loving which I think is very important.

After my dad retired from football, he wanted me to move to Minnesota with him. I was going into the sixth grade and had to move to a new city and surroundings. I left my grandparents' home and cousin and it was just my dad and me from then on. I was nervous and a bit anxious. I loved my dad but had never lived with him, so I wasn't sure how things would work. We lived in a nice suburb called Eden Prairie. At the time, Eden Prairie felt like it was 99.99999% white, which was an adjustment for me. Not that I grew up in the inner city, but I always had more than one race around me. Sometimes being the son of a former Viking helped me get through the race challenges a little easier than other black kids in the area. My dad just wanted me to focus on school and try not to pay attention to the racial divide. But now when I look back, I find it funny how little diversity was in Minnesota and Eden Prairie at that time. Now it seems like another world because there is a lot more diversity there than I could have ever imagined.

Probably one of my favorite pictures of me and my dad.
We formed a special bond early on and it continues to this day.

Dad always put a big emphasis on academics. He was always harder on me academically than in sports. Middle school was an adjustment for me. I think some kids were jealous of me because of who my dad was. Eighth graders knocked me around often. I remember walking down the hall with a handful of books when a hockey player threw me into a plexiglass wall. My books flew everywhere as people laughed. I was the talk of the school for the first few weeks, even though it felt like a full year. I was tall and skinny without much confidence. I was scared and there were very few African American kids in school. I knew I couldn't act out physically, but through sports I could channel the animosity I was forming. I was mad that I had to move, I was mad that I didn't have both of my parents around, and I was mad that I wasn't a part of the in-crowd. I was jealous of people who had their parents at their games or who had things I didn't have.

I turned this aggression into playing football. I learned how to hide my emotions because that's what I thought real men did, at least the men in my family did. Even though football was my outlet, basketball was my first love.

Putting the finishing touches on a birthday dunk against a cross town rival. Basketball was my first love but I knew football was my future. Short shorts and hops.

Another fond memory is when my Aunt Helen and I used to watch the NBA finals. We definitely used to cheer for the Lakers to beat the Celtics. Our favorite player was Michael Cooper also known as "Cooper Looper" in our house. We lived and died on every basket. I didn't have a real reason to like the Lakers except that I liked Michael Cooper's socks. He would pull up his tall white socks to his knees almost.

I enjoyed time with my Aunt Helen. I would go down to her house in Minneapolis on the weekends. I learned a lot there, how to street ball, and how to survive I also had a connection to my mom even though she was thousands of miles away.

I lived for the weekends when I would go see my mom's sister, Aunt Helen Marie, and my cousins, O.V. and Chandra.

O.V. became like a big brother to me and Chandra and I had a bond that was natural - we have the same birthday. They lived in the inner city, south side of Minneapolis. I would talk to my mom all weekend because I had more access to her from there. Culturally, I got to see a whole different perspective and point of view. I learned to fend for myself and ate a lot of soul food. After a good NBA game, I would go out to the park and pretend to be anyone from Larry Bird to Dr. J. I played basketball with anyone in the hood and learned to problem-solve on the court, with words and actions. I toughened up on my weekend visits and saw how life really was outside of the sheltered confines of the suburbs. My dad used to always tell me I was going down to Minneapolis to get "brother-ized."

Sounds somewhat funny but it was true. It was there that I learned how to throw hands. I took a few losses in the beginning but always came back to even the score. I came back more out of fear of being a chump or embarrassed. Life lessons accrue no matter what age or place you are in.

My dad played football during a time when players weren't making huge amounts of money, mainly because there wasn't any free agency, but they seemed to have more pure and good times than modern day players do or can. There was no social media or having to live life in a bubble. My dad and I have talked plenty of times about how he nor his guys never had to worry about women trying to "trap" them, etc., as they all wanted to have a good time. One very real conversation we had was about women and how they could be a man's downfall. He always said, "Do as I say, not as I do." It took a good person to realize his faults and try and point me into the right direction. One thing he did was try to hide me from all the negative things, which for me was both good and bad. By not seeing it or talking about it, I drew my own conclusions. One thing I respect about my dad is that he never brought anyone around me until they were serious.

The one that was "serious" was a lady named Beverly Cahn. She was around the majority of my childhood. She was a truly selfless person, a great mother figure for me, and always loved and treated me as her own. She and my dad dated for what seemed like most of my childhood until I was sixteen, I think. As a result, with all the other things going on, I always loved being with her and especially when her and my dad were together. She was in my life until one day my dad sat me down and told me Beverly had left him for good.

The break up wasn't easy on me, because as a teenager I had no idea of the dynamics of a relationship, let alone anything about life. Hell, I was just getting peach fuzz on my balls and that was a big deal to me back then. I do know that in the late 80's and early 90's it wasn't always acceptable when dealing with a mixed couple. But regardless, I was angry at her, my dad and everyone else. Right then I began to focus on getting out of the house, not because I hated it but because all that I knew was gone and I thought the best thing to do was to run. The one good thing that came out of it was that I learned of two other siblings I had. Mainly, I think my dad realized I was mature enough to grasp the situation. I think he perceived that I let the fact of Beverly leaving roll off my shoulders, but little did he know, I had so much turmoil inside I almost couldn't take it. The new siblings weren't a factor in the break up but soon became a factor in my life which put me into a weird spot. I think at that age I felt I was already walking around trying to find myself and I sure as hell didn't know how to communicate with a stranger at that time.

**My cousin O.V., that smile says it all. Homeboy
was always the life of the party.
We had good and bad times, but he's family.**

Two

Growth

As I grew older, I got more confident and skilled in my athleticism. I went to Eden Prairie High School in ninth grade where I flourished in football and basketball. I was a running back. It was a natural position for me. I was head and shoulders above the other kids. Physically, I was advanced and strong, socially, I was awkward. I had big feet and skinny legs with a big head. My uncle Gary used to call me "Egg Head." I was shy, but regardless if I became popular on the field, I felt more comfortable with the nerds or kids with issues. I always thought to myself, "I should treat everyone the same, because you never know what they have going on or what they could become."

Through football, I was able to find a release. I had anxiety from the moment I woke up in the morning, going through the whole day of school, trying to fit in and not feel out of place. Once I was on the field, I never felt a thing. I let go of all the anxiety and frustration on the field. I knew in that small realm on the field, I was the king. I was shy, but in football, I was outgoing and aggressive. It was like a "Dr. Jekyll and Mr. Hyde" mentality to my everyday life. As I look back, I think it came from not having my siblings around and also having to be aware of other kids and their intentions, which makes a young person become an introvert.

Regardless of how well I did in football or basketball, the sport of choice at the time was hockey. Since I didn't play, I always felt a lot of tension from some of the hockey players, and because I was one of the only black students on campus, I felt even more irrelevant. At times, it seemed some of the hockey players or coaches were racially inappropriate. They would wear hockey jerseys to school with their nicknames on the back. One kid wore a jersey with the nickname "Grand Wizard" on the back. I was instantly sick to my stomach, as it was common knowledge at the time that the leader of the KKK was known as the "Grand Wizard." I knew it was the suburbs and there were not many people of color at the school, but that was the straw that broke the camel's back in some way. That day, the six or seven other black kids at the school and I went off in a full blown riot with the hockey team. Many kids acted like they had no idea about the racial divide, but whether it was true or not, they learned that day. There are always times in life when you have to step up and be accounted for or you will let people run over you forever. Sadly, that fight gave me more confidence to stick up for not only myself but for things that weren't right regardless of color or race.

Here's a tip: *A man that is indifferent is a coward and cannot be trusted because you will never know where he stands, but a man with an opinion, even if it's different than yours, is someone you can work with because you know where he stands!*

Later that year, my coach yelled to me, "Get your monkey ass over here." My dad was done. He would put up with a lot of the ignorance at times, but he was not going to have me go to a school that was outright disrespectful. I transferred to Minnetonka High School for tenth and eleventh grade. Even though I grew up in Eden Prairie, when I went to Minnetonka, Eden Prairie's cross town rival, I made more life-long friends. One of the guys I met was Jamal Lewis who I also referred to as my main "nigga behind the trigga." I knew Jamal prior from competing in sports but never on a personal level. Who knew we'd end up like brothers to this day? He and his family welcomed me with open arms.

Funny fact: Until 1999, my real name was Jamal Antoine Lewis but everyone knew me as Jamal (Jay) Foreman. My mom had my name on the original birth certificate as Lewis, probably because my dad wasn't there or had pissed her off. When my dad got custody he went to change my name but never finished the paper work or paid for it. Crazy how life works isn't it? Better yet, crazy how God works. Little did I know that my friend Jamal Lewis would act more like "family" than my own flesh and blood.

There were more African Americans at Minnetonka, and I felt I had a safe place to grow as a young man and learn. I developed lifelong friendships and cultivated confidence that would steer me towards my goals. I worked hard in tenth and eleventh grades, on and off the field. It was during that time that I started looking at football as a business decision. I was starting on Varsity with football. Brian Cohen, my team-mate, was going through the recruiting process and talked to me about it. He told me what to focus on and what not to focus on. It was then that I decided I might have a chance to play football in college and get my degree at the same time. My dad was on board, and I formulated a goal of playing football in college for a scholarship. I wanted the best educa-tion and to make something of myself. I created my own luck and took advantage of the opportunities that were there. Sometimes kids in high school forget to think about their future because they are so caught up in the now. They do not realize their decisions could alter their futures and have life-long consequences.

I knew I was playing in every game, which was more of an opportu-nity for scouts to watch me and offer me a scholarship. I was determined to make it happen. I knew I would need to have exceptional grades to get a scholarship as well. I will say though that I never liked school. I thought I was smart, but I was never an "advanced student." Like most people, I would never have reached the height of my career without the help of people who truly saw something special in me.

One of those people was the school librarian, Phyllis Knapp, who helped me with school. She looked over my schedule and tutored me before school and after practices. She taught me about time management and sacrifice before I ever understood what they even were. By my junior year, my GPA went up drastically and I knew I had a real chance of going to a big college. My coach didn't agree. It seemed to me that he didn't really believe I had what it took to go to a Division One college. During my junior year, if I were killing it in a game, he would randomly bench me. I was very confused on what fueled his decisions but didn't have time to figure it out. For some reason, he wasn't trying to play me, and when I would talk about Division One schools, he would make comments on how I should just be happy with what I got.

Even with all the good going on at Minnetonka, I chose to transfer back to Eden Prairie High School. This was the first big decision in my life and sports career. Do I stay with my friends and take a chance of not reaching my goals? Or, do I make a personal decision and find out who my real friends are? I chose the latter. I realized sometimes you have to look out for yourself first because most times nobody else will. One thing I was told by a family member was, "Nobody will love Jay Foreman like Jay Foreman will." My dad knew the same. By the end of the season he transferred me back to Eden Prairie for the remainder of my eleventh grade and senior years. By this time, they had a new coach, Mike Grant, who was also a huge reason I went back. He was a tremendous influence on me, on and off the field, in achieving my Division One goal.

We knew I had a real chance of getting a scholarship. Coach Grant, along with my dad, were so instrumental in helping me focus and set out a plan. Even though I was a great high school player, I still had an uphill battle to make a name for myself. I felt I was definitely one of the best players in the state, yet the University of Minnesota coach, Jim Wacker, didn't want to give me a chance. I took it to heart. I knew I was better than every kid he was recruiting and it spurred me to work harder. I started getting letters from Michigan State, Arizona State, Notre Dame, but kids need to understand that there is a big difference in letters and offers. I learned that the hard way.

Aunt Helen, Nanny, and me at my High School graduation. These two always pushed me to do better and to think on my own.

I knew if I had a great senior year I could very likely achieve my goals. My coach primed me to be a leader. At first, I struggled because I was so focused on past high school experiences that I forgot the present. I quickly retracted and got re-focused to really think about my team and put my team first. I knew I had to do right by them to really get where I wanted. I had a great senior year. One game against Bloomington Jefferson, Coach Grant came to me and pointed out that Nebraska was there to watch three guys on the opposing team. On that rival team was, Lane Kiffin. Lane has now made a name for himself in the coaching ranks as a Head Coach and some for his brash personality. I'll tell you, deep down Lane is a good dude. We were ball boys for the Minnesota Vikings for two training camps as his dad was coaching for them. Bloomington Jefferson was mainly known for hockey, but also whose students were known for being a bunch of preppy, stuck-up punks. I'll admit they always had good athletes though. In fact, that year they had three Division One recruits - Lane, Lloyd Lee and Dave Watson.

I knew if I wanted a scholarship with Nebraska, I had my opportunity during that game with Bloomington Jefferson. I went to the bathroom and psyched myself up. I was ready to take a scholarship from those kids who the recruiters were there to see. There wasn't a play where I didn't kill it. I was easily the most dominant player in the game. This was the opportunity my grandpa talked about. I kicked the door in and let those recruiters know my name. I managed to knock two guys out of the game and the Nebraska recruiters quickly learned my phone number and called every week. In fact, the coach that was calling me was Dan Young. Coach Young had to be the most monotone person I ever heard but he was very consistent. He called every Monday night at around 6:30 PM always asking about my stats and going over a play or two from the previous game. Back then they had to have tapes mailed so they didn't see the most recent game until the following week.

At the end of the season, I had several colleges that wanted me to visit - University of Miami, University of Iowa, Nebraska, Wyoming, and Wisconsin as well as a few others in the Big Ten and Big Eight. I knew I wasn't going to accept any invitations unless I knew they were going to offer a full scholarship. I went to Wyoming because my buddy Marcus Harris played there. He was a good friend of mine and I really just wanted to visit him for free. It was the most fun visit, by far, as we played with snowmobiles and went to the shooting range. I never really considered them, so it was more like an extravaganza than a serious visit. The University of Iowa recruited me early. Iowa was a school and team I had been eyeing because I saw instant playing time, and also, for the foolish reason that the father of my high school girlfriend went there.

Lesson: *Never think with the small head.*

I visited the University of Iowa and was almost ready to commit. I think I felt like this because, at the time, they were the first big school to offer a scholarship and I didn't have any experience with other options. Overall, the visit went well, but something was holding me back from giving them my word. Behold, the feeling I had been having had come to light. It was only a few minutes before I was to head to the airport when the coach stopped the tape we were watching in regards to my competition and dropped a bomb. He tried to explain to me that since my ACT score was a 24, it didn't match up with my GPA and class ranking. That meant I would have to go to class in the summer but not get any grades. I was hurt and disappointed, but deep down I said, "HELL NO!!" After that, offers and visits came flooding in. It was during that time I visited the University of Nebraska. I didn't know much about the school, but could tell immediately that they had a great fan base as well as a stellar academic program. Besides the academics, they had a deep tradition and were on the upswing. Mainly, I associated the Huskers with always getting their asses beat by a Florida team on New Year's Day. I grew up in a Miami house so we laughed at the Huskers, but that season was a magical year for them. They took Florida State to the woodshed but came up short on a missed field goal.

To be transparent, one thing on my mind as a recruit was getting laid by a college girl.   Nebraska didn't disappoint. They had a winning team, strength program, academics and straight up freaks. I was taken to a house party that lasted all night long, and even my corny ass pulled a chick. I remember her being fine as hell, and we hooked up both nights I was there. I would say Nebraska took the lead because of that alone.

The only bad recruiting experience I had was when I visited the University of Wisconsin. At that time, Wisconsin was on a magical Rose Bowl run. It was close to home, and a few Minnesota kids had gone there. The only rule my dad had about college invitations was if a college invited me for a visit, a scholarship offer was going to be part of it. Coach Alvarez contacted me and confirmed the trip and offer. Wisconsin was my first visit and I was excited. We went to a frat party and got our party on.

We had lunch at Coach Alvarez's house the next morning; he had a nice pad. After talking with others on the trip and the various coaches that were there, each player was called into his office. I was thinking I might commit to them on the trip. Little did I know what was about to happen. I got called into his office and we started with small talk and then discussed the Rose Bowl. He asked me what I wanted to major in and what other schools were considering me. Of course I told him which schools. He turned to me and said, "Sounds like you have some great options." I thought, "What the hell?" Then he said, "We can't offer you a scholarship right now. Would you be interested in walking on?" I not so politely rejected his offer, told him to "F*** off," and asked to leave. At the airport, I used the four quarters my dad always told me to have and I called home. My dad answered, I told him what happened and he was irate. I think the next time Wisconsin called, he cussed the coach out for ten minutes and hung up. Needless to say, they never called again. This is why I will always have anger toward Wisconsin.

It was later in the middle of the national championships, when Coach Osborne showed up at my house to discuss my options with the University of Nebraska, that I realized how much faith he had that I would be a great asset for his team. He told me from day one that even if I got hurt, he would still honor my scholarship. He gave me his word, and I gave mine. I had done it. I committed to not only a Division One school, but also the University of Nebraska, a national title championship school. I was going to the University of Nebraska on a full scholarship. I always say that Miami was my first choice but didn't go there because of the probation. Iowa was the second choice, but when Hayden Frye didn't bother to make an in-home visit when a national championship team's head coach did, I knew that wasn't the place for me. It's the little things that lead to big things.

Things to look for when choosing a college:

1. How long has the coach been there?
2. How long and hard have they worked to recruit you?

3. Is there anyone from your area that has studied there or played for any of the coaches?

4. Can you see yourself living there after you play there? Whether you are a starter or bench warmer you have to build a foundation for when football ends. Guys that move back home most likely wasted a lot of time at their school. 1% of NCAA football players make it to the NFL and it won't change.

5. What type of support do they offer academically and socially? This is huge for African American athletes going to places where they are one of few.

6. What type of offense or defense do they run and does it fit your skill set?

7. Pick a position on offense or defense that you could play, most likely the position you played in high school.

8. How far is it from home? 99% of kids get homesick within the first two years. It's always good to have your support system close by.

9. What is the campus social life like? A look into the social life on campus outside of your sport is crucial. Why? Because that is most likely the people you will be working with, against and for in your real life career. One thing to look at is if there is diversity on campus. If you are not sure, make sure you ask. Don't forget to ask about the programs they have for kids in the same situation or close to it.

Three

Proving Ground

It was 1994 and I was so ready for college. I was ready to emerge from my dad's shadow and start building a name for myself in a new area. It was like a reset button for me. I created my own type of normal, although I was keenly aware that there would be challenges waiting for me. I saw so many athletes that did well in high school flame out in college because they couldn't hack it socially, mentally, or emotionally and let it affect their athletic ability. I felt that since I was one of the best athletes in the state, I probably didn't have to work as hard as others.

The summer before college, Nebraska sent me a workout package for the offseason. I tossed it in the garbage and hung out with my friends and girlfriend while working a part time job at the grocery store and enjoying my last months of freedom before school started. I knew I wasn't going to play as much as a freshman, so I didn't feel the pressure that I would years later. In reality, I think I did so because I was scared of what was to come. All I ever heard from friends and Nebraska fans was how hard they worked and how much they lifted weights. I knew in my head, no matter what, I wouldn't embarrass myself and wouldn't quit. But is not giving 100% the same as quitting? Smart money says maybe so. All my athletic years I was told I'd be a late bloomer and that I needed time. I guess that was stuck in my mind in regards to my last few weeks of freedom.

It wasn't until a week before I was supposed to move to Nebraska that I thought I should start working out hard. My friend Jamal helped me practice a 300-yard shuttle. I didn't pass the first two times, but got it two days before leaving. In the packet that Nebraska sent us it said that it "was strongly encouraged" to pass the 300-yard shuttle. The 300-yard shuttle is a sprint to the fifty-yard line and back to the goal line in a certain amount of time. Seems easy right? It is until that monkey jumps on your back about the second time down and back. The time had come for me to leave. I said goodbye to my friends and girlfriend as well as cousin and aunt. I was ready to head south. The funny part is that I was so sprung in high school that I thought I'd end up marrying my high school girlfriend Alexis. She was an athlete herself and came from a great family. Great breeding material if you ask me. She was a stallion way before her time. When I look back, I think I learned a lot of what I thought a life and family should be based on my friends' families and what I saw on TV. Lucky for me that T.V. back then wasn't nearly as extreme as it is now. So maybe I was a hopeless romantic at heart without even knowing it. Regardless, it was time for me to start this new phase of my life.

My dad drove me, and it was a nice ride as I was charged and eager to get there - until we passed the Nebraska state line. My dad turned down the radio and said, "Enough of the bullshit… now listen, your last name is Foreman… your great grandfather did this, your grandfather did this…. when you go in, you don't quit. Don't back down from a challenge, and remember the sacrifices your ancestors made to get you this far… and lastly, don't you bring your black ass home without a degree. If you get in trouble to the point I have to come down here because of it, I will kick your ass." He slowly turned the music back up as I sat there in shock and a bit uncomfortable. I had thought I would go to college and have fun. I thought all the girls from the recruiting visit would be there waiting for me and I would play some college football - but now, I realized there was so much more riding on this experience. This was my chance to make something out of myself, make my family proud and create a future. I was excited and terrified at the same time.

I got to the campus, which looked so different than the recruiting visit, and the girls were NOT lined up to greet me. There was so much hustle and bustle of students moving in. Anxiety mixed with enthusiasm seemed to have taken over the campus. I got my dorm set up and my dad left. I didn't know what I was supposed to do then. I was officially on my own and able to make my own choices.

Me as a freshman.
I didn't know what I was doing but was sure happy to be there.
I weighed between 185-190 pounds when I left high school.
When I left college I was easily 235-240 pounds.
Amazing what three square meals and some weights can do!!!

All the freshmen ball players got together, sized each other up and talked about the recruiting visits. Each one of us had the hopeful anticipation of being stars for Nebraska, but the reality was that not many of us would make it to the end of the program. Looking back at that time, there were very few that made it along-side me.

The first couple of days we each got a full physical and checked out the campus, all while mentally noting that we were competing against one another. We all started questioning everyone, trying to figure out who was going to play where, who was coming in, where they came from, how good they were in high school or in freshmen practice. Our first week of practice was high school level. We practiced for three days to get used to the intensity. Just going against each other was like the All-Star game on steroids. It wasn't until later when the veterans arrived at practice, that things were really put into perspective. I kept thinking how I was totally out of place and I shouldn't have thrown the summer workouts in the trash. These guys were in great physical condition; they were faster than me and bigger than me.

At one point we were all sitting together waiting for a meeting. I looked down at the weight room where a guy came out built like Arnold Schwarzenegger. He was about 6'3", 310 pounds, wearing short daisy duke style jean shorts and a small pink Gold's Gym tank top. His hair was slicked back and he came right up to our group and said, "Look at you, you are a bunch of f****** babies!" He went down the line pointing to each one of us and said, "You're a pussy… you're a pussy…. you're a pussy… I'm your worst nightmare!" Being raised by alpha-males and forming my own ego, I wasn't bothered by anything he said. I spoke out and replied, "Who are you, the weight coach or what?"

He walked over to me and said, "I'm Christian Peter, f****** starting nose tackle, you, stupid freshman!" Everyone was silent, including me until he left.

We had to wait to check in with coaches. My coach was Tony Samuels. I was with three other freshmen but was held for a while, so when I went to the auditorium for our first meeting, everyone else already had their seat. In the whole auditorium, there was one seat left - next to Christian Peter. I sat next to him and he put his arm around me and yelled out, "I got a cute little bitch this year." I had to sit next to Christian for the entire year.

I was outwardly confident but inwardly super intimidated.

It was time for our first real practice and things were getting tough. I was on the practice squad going against the first team offense. It was a game simulation and the speed and strength was nothing like I knew. I found myself questioning if I really deserved to be there. I was fortunate to have my dad as a sounding board on days when I would question myself. I was so used to being the best on the team, best in the school, best in the conference, and best in the state. Now I was getting tossed around left and right. I had to remember to keep it simple. If you keep things simple you can't do a lot of stupid things, don't throw the negatives away, focus on the positive - these were the things my dad would advise me. It worked. My whole first year, I did well at practice, sometimes out performing guys that played on Saturdays. I was a redshirt freshman and excited to form a plan to make up for the time I may have lost. I watched an hour to two hours of film daily. I had a goal and was not only competing with my teammates for a spot, but also myself. Long before the season was over I saw that there would be a huge opportunity to play because of the departure of the top two guys that were seniors.

We won the National Championship that year and as exciting as that was for everyone, I just kept thinking that there would be more people wanting to come to Nebraska to play. I had a lot to prove to get a spot, especially when the number one linebacker in the nation signed two days later. His name was Tony Ortiz and he was a big track and football star in Connecticut. Even though I was a little nervous, I would have helped him in any way because I wanted to do what was best for the team. It's hard to understand and be prepared for that fight at eighteen or nineteen years old but you have to learn to trust the "process." The good ole' process is coach terms for letting the chips fall where they may.

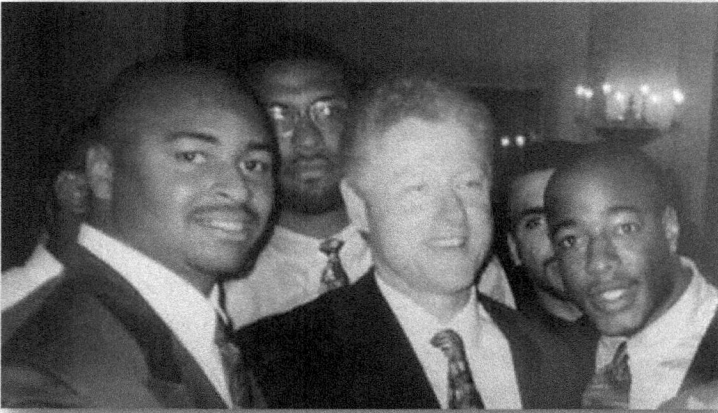

L to R: Me, Mike Rucker, Tony Ortiz, President Bill Clinton, Jay Gates
I was surprised at how tall President Clinton was, how he
actually talked to all of us, asked about where we were
from, and wanted to know about our families.
I will always remember that.

I was in the weight room constantly. I never took time off in the off-season. I didn't party too much but would stay in the dorms and focus on eating to gain weight and working out to build muscle. I knew I needed to make it hard to beat me. I wanted to be more prepared than anyone else, smarter and mentally tougher than anyone on my team.

My uncle would call me often and rebuild confidence in me during the times I was tired. He would tell me if I wasn't confident, I would be an easy target. He had a way of mentally training me that clicked.

During spring ball, *The Daily Nebraskan* had a sports section for our spring ball depth chart. I wasn't even on the depth chart. I felt defeated for a minute, but remembered I had a lot to prove. I started at number six, and stuck to the plan. After the first week of outworking everyone, I was number four, and the second week I was number three.

I ended spring ball at number one. I was suddenly getting articles written about me with the questions like, "Who is this kid? He wasn't on the depth chart at all and now he was listed as a starter?" It's never where you start, but where you finish. I remember a fan coming up to me after being in the NFL awhile and saying, "Don't take this the wrong way, but when I saw you as a sophomore in high school you weren't that good. I followed you throughout high school and college and man, you really busted onto the scene and developed." I didn't know whether to hug this man or punch him in the face.

The final step for that spring was the Spring Game. Most colleges' spring games are just like a regular practice. Not at Nebraska! Nebraska is well known for its fans and boy did they come out for that game. I heard about the fans, but I was shocked when a player said there might be close to 60,000 people there. I won't lie, I almost shit my pants. I didn't shit my pants, but I was daydreaming about the game and got drilled in the face with a ball and my nose was bleeding like a faucet. The only good thing was that I had blood on my pants and jersey so at least I looked tough. I had never been in a game this big in my life. It's different watching versus actually playing in it. I knew positions were won and lost in this game and I was determined to show everyone that what they have been reading was for real and I wasn't a punk.

**It was a true honor to lead these guys. I was a small piece in the big puzzle.
Left to right: Me, Eric Johnson, Grant Wistrom and Jason Peter**

As the game approached, I felt alone. I was on the first team but none of my other classmates were and no one had a chance to even start. On the other hand, all the upper class guys were looking at me to see what I was going to do, plus I was still in the north stadium locker room. I chose to approach it as any other practice and just to go out and play hard. I knew the defense and I knew I could find the ball, which is what I did to the tune of fifteen tackles. That was it. I had balls the size of grapefruits and nobody could tell me otherwise.

Guidance for success in college:

1. Be on time.
2. Be accountable.
3. Be available.
4. Shut up and show up.
5. Let your actions do the talking.
6. Model yourself after someone that has done what you strive to do.
7. Be careful who you hang with and where you hang out.
8. There is no girl worth your career, life or scholarship.
9. Bro's before hoes.
10. Use condoms no matter who she is.

Four

A Place at the Table

After a long summer, I began to realize that sitting next to Christian Peter all year in meetings had some advantages. He ended up giving me great advice here and there. One piece of advice was to make sure to enroll for summer school. The class sizes were smaller and teachers were more available to work one- on-one with the students. I decided to do that and stay focused and regimented on school and working out during the summer before my second year, but I couldn't shake the idea of having a new kid come in and try to take my spot.

My dad overheard a coach talking about it too and wouldn't hesitate to taunt me with it. He knew how to annoy me and motivate me at the same time. He would yell at me saying, "This kid needs to come in and earn it, not have it given to him." It drove me even harder when he would tell me not to let him come take my job. He would say, "Your last name is Foreman and you are no punk. If he is going to get your spot he's going to have to beat you out. You aren't going to let him do that are you?" Those words ran through my head I bet a hundred times a day.

There were ten guys coming in as starters, and red shirt freshmen listed as starters. I hadn't played in a game since high school. I had a lot to prove to everyone that I deserved to be there and had earned my spot, all while knowing the elephant in the room was about this number one linebacker in the country. I couldn't wait for my day against him.

I remember meeting Tony who had huge hype and accolades coming into the program. It probably wasn't the best thing for him because it put the spotlight on him from the get go. I think he, along with Ahman Green, were some of the biggest recruits Nebraska had landed in some time. When the time came, I realized he was fast and had a ton of potential, but I was mentally more prepared and familiar with what we were doing so I had the advantage. The things he was learning or adjusting to, I had been through plenty of times before. The hardest thing to do in the transition from high school to college was to realize that no matter how good you were in high school it didn't matter once you got to college. The expectations are so much higher in major college sports that I think kids can get overwhelmed by it. I didn't want to make the transition harder for him, but I knew I was better than him at the time. Regardless of competition, I became great friends with Tony and still look at him and love him like a brother. I would never turn my back on a teammate. NEVER! I actually grew to appreciate Tony a lot, but I think at first he didn't like that I was playing over him. Instead of being mad about that, I looked at it as a positive situation because I knew eventually I could trust him on the field. I saw how hard he was willing to work even when things didn't work out for him.

Even though I was running with the starters, I was not in the north locker room yet. Any freshman or other players who hadn't been in the program for a full year had the south locker room with steel lockers that were rusted and smelled. There was barely any hot water. We called it the "dungeon." The urinals were old and if anyone had to go to the bathroom, there were no doors. It was part of the process. After two days, we ended up in the south locker room, where all the equipment guys moved our stuff and gave us a locker. Before we were able to walk in the locker room, we had to line up in alphabetical order and get called in one at a time where we would get doused with water and baby powder and hit with a whiffle ball bat.   It was the "welcome" to the nice locker room. That was the extent of any hazing. Even though I had a little case of the red ass, I enjoyed it because I was on the varsity team.

Even though we were a little scared, we all looked forward to the better locker room and the cross over. I had a locker next to Aaron Penland and Phil Ellis. Phil was a Nebraska kid from a small town out west called Grand Island. He was about 6'1" and weighed 215 pounds but was tough as nails and smart on the field. He would never blow your socks off running in shorts, but when homeboy got on the field he had tremendous game speed.

Aaron Penland was a nutcase. He had these huge, heavy hands and always wanted to wrestle or rough you up. I think he had two or three older brothers, so he was in heaven when he was around the guys. He was the kind of guy that the offense hated to practice against, because he never took it easy and would laugh when he'd light someone up. Needless to say, I learned a lot from both of them even though I was the complete opposite person and player. The great thing about them was that they took me under their wings and showed me how to work, gave me confidence, and got me to play as physical as I could. I was excited about our upcoming season.

Our first game of the season was against Oklahoma State. As ready as I was, I got anxious and a bit nervous as the game got closer. I was comfortable practicing against my teammates in practice, but I knew I was going to be tested in the game. I hadn't played since high school and was suddenly flooded with doubt again. I questioned if I was really ready and could hang with everyone else. A quick call from my uncle and dad as well as remembering what my grandpa always told me got me excited and ready to leave my mark and make people remember my name.

I was hyped, and during the first play of the game, I got validated. They ran the ball at me, and I knew no matter what, I was not going to get run over. I blew up the full back and tackled the running back for a five-yard loss. Everyone else was more excited than I was. To me it was a sigh of relief that I could play at this level and still had it in me.

In college football and sometimes life, you only get one or two chances to play. To take advantage of that opportunity when it comes, you have to be ready - mind, soul and body. I was relieved when the game was over. I played decent and realized that season was going to be a test and was going to get me stronger for the following year.

We had a great season that year, but we had some hiccups to get to the National Championship. We had some issues off the field that were challenging to get through. The one that has never left the program was after we went to play Michigan State. It was a huge game because they were ranked top five in the nation. We played and beat the brakes off of them on the road. Our best player, Lawrence Phillips, ripped MSU a new asshole and put the whole nation on notice that he was head and shoulders better than anyone else, regardless of position. After games, players go their own way, and long story short, Lawrence got into some serious shit over his then girlfriend and some other player on the team. He got arrested and suspended from the team until late in the year. It brought so much bad attention to the program that we had more media at practices and games than I bet the Kansas City Chiefs did that year. Even after all that, the very next weekend we had a tight-end get accused of sexual assault and other players had issues at bars while intoxicated. It seemed like we were doomed to fuck up a magical team and season, but I will say, that year was probably Coach Osborne's best coaching job even though I'm sure he hated it. We had some strong leaders who put a nix to anyone going out downtown or the bars for the rest of the season. That took some serious nuts, but there wasn't one guy who balked at it.

The Lawrence Phillips situation was always something I looked at as a mistake. Not that what he did was right, but I always felt like he never got to tell his side of the story. For as much media attention that was there to bash him, the university, and Coach Osborne, I felt it was unjust for the media to not do their research and get all the facts, not to condone Lawrence's actions, but to shed light on the whole night and season. I was not close with Lawrence; we had mutual respect and he is by far one of the best running backs I ever went against.

I remember after we played Oklahoma in his first game back, he needed a ride to his car. I was in the car with my dad, Lawrence and Clinton Childs. I'll never forget Lawrence telling us that all he ever wanted was an adult figure to love him. I sat there thinking, "Damn, I didn't even know people didn't have that, or better yet, Lawrence had that much emotion built up in him." I truly felt sorry for him, because he never had the basics that every child should have. Whether it was handled right or wrong, I always felt he didn't get his fair shake from the media or people who should have helped him beyond the white lines. To their defense, if Lawrence didn't want to hear it he wouldn't. I'll always have fond memories of him.

That season was not only the best but the hardest. We were ready for the opportunity to play for the National Championship though. We had so many pent up, outside distractions and all of us needed to release them on the field. Nebraska was known as a big running team, a physical team. Florida was known to pass the ball 70% of the time. Florida's main game plan was to intimidate us. We practiced hard for two weeks prior to the game. Florida didn't practice until they got there, which was only seven days before the game. We took that as a sign of disrespect and wanted to make it as physical as we could for them.

There was so much emotion going into that game. I think it was the first National Championship game when the top two teams were playing. We were in warm ups, stretching before the game, when Florida decided to run right through our line-up, kicking our helmets. A fight broke out and that was all we needed to get motivated to win that game. We beat them with a score of 62-24 and won the National Championship. Our 1995 Nebraska team was arguably one of the top two college teams ever. I ended up being third or fourth on the team in tackles. Even with all the instant success, I was not happy with myself, or my role. I was raised to be hard but fair and get what you earned, and I felt I earned my starting position through my play and hard work.

Outside of football, I was enjoying college life. I dated a girl named Jane. Even though I didn't grow up in a two-parent home or with a constant daily female figure, I always thought I would meet a girl and fall in love and have the whole white picket fence house thing with a couple of kids and a dog. I was head over heels for Jane. I liked her a lot, and contrary to my regular habits, I trusted her.

When I found out Jane was also dating a few of my teammates, it hardened me against women a little more. I was so impressionable at that age, and the fact that she was seeing my friends behind my back was too much. I actually liked her, and they were just taking advantage of an easy situation. I reflected on various times I would see my dad's experiences with women, always resulting in the fact that they couldn't be trusted. It became a defense mechanism for me to deal with them. But in reality, it was a good learning experience and it was college life.

I wanted control in so many areas. As a child, I didn't have control of my parents or mother figure or actions. In my late teens I just wanted stability and tried to control every aspect of my life. Football seemed like the only thing I could control until I heard early in my offseason that the coaches were changing my position, from outside linebacker to middle linebacker. I had worked so hard to earn my spot as an outside line-backer, and now had to start all over again to get notoriety as a middle linebacker. I was shocked! Now I was going to have to compete with a guy who was already penciled in to start. My initial reaction was to transfer to a different school. I was young and a hot head of sorts but I felt that they were doing me wrong. I had feelers to Notre Dame, Georgia, Michigan and a few other schools. If any, I was headed to Michigan because my good friend Jason Kapsner was there and I had spoken to him a few times to see what it was like.

It was my first time dealing with politics in big time sports. I had no idea what to do until my dad came down to have a sit- down with me. He helped break it down for me and told me that every time I faced ad-versity in sports, I couldn't just leave. I was in a leadership position, and even though it wasn't right, I had the opportunity to start. I just needed to take the emotion out of it and remember I was there to also get a degree. Nebraska was a good school, and I decided I would stick it out and start over again. There was so much turmoil right after the National Championship and coaches heard the rumblings. Coach Osborne talked to me as well and that seemed to have a calming effect on me. He made a commitment that as long as I committed to making myself bigger, faster and stronger, he would commit to giving me every chance to play a starting position.

He created an internal anger for me to use the right way and I used much of the offseason training for spring ball to make some sort of comeback for myself. I was told I had a fair chance to start at middle linebacker BUT soon realized the position was promised to a local kid from Lincoln named Jon Hesse. Jon was a big kid who played safety in high school and had some ability.

I'll never say he was better, but he was cool enough to tell me Coach Bohl had promised him he'd start long before I had a chance to even practice.

Five

ADVERSITY STRIKES

It seemed like my phone was constantly ringing during the offseason. My dad and uncle were calling to check on me. "How's your weight? How's practice? How are you doing with school?" I hated answering the phone when they called. It was also during this time my grandfather's health started failing. I felt like I never got good news in regards to him, so answering the phone was always stressful, whether it was about football or my grandfather. It was a tense time personally for me and for us as a team overall.

Our quarterback, Tommy Frazier, graduated and Scott Frost transferred in to take his place. It was going to be quite a transition year for us. Scott seemed cocky, and a lot of guys had animosity toward him coming in. Scott was given a starting spot which made some players feel like he didn't have to work for it like others did. There was a lack of respect growing amongst the team and it soon became divided. To Scott's defense, he was put into a no win situation. If he didn't win all the games, he was a failure. If he won them all, then that's what he should have done. To be honest, what player, more specifically, what quarterback isn't cocky? To me, the cockier, the better. Sometimes I think being cocky can be taken too far or misunderstood. I think in Scott's case it was a little of both. I never had an issue with him at all. Nobody is perfect in college anyways.

Three main qualities a coach and teammate looks for in a player:

1. Can they trust you? Trusting another player is huge because that trust is what you depend on when you need to pull out those hard fought victories.
2. Do they like you? Now this is tricky, because people mistake liking you with being a politician. Not the case, being liked means you purposely aren't a jerk.
3. Do they respect you? Some of the greatest players that ever played at Nebraska and the NFL were respected as players. This is huge because football players can look past who you are personally as long as you can make plays and be a good teammate on the field.

We had a lot of national press and our team was in turmoil. Guys were partying and getting into trouble. There was a lack of leadership since so many guys were leaving and the new morale was faltering. The summer before season, there was a party at my house and drinks were flowing. Someone got into a fight and the girlfriend of one player ended up being pushed in the middle of the fight. That one event felt like it separated the team and created the divide that would follow us into the season that year. We had so much discord and there was nothing I felt I could do to better the situation.

I decided I wanted to find ways to do what was best for the team and wanted to help the players strive in their positions while being a backbone and leader and trying to bring the team together. As much as I wanted to help, I struggled with my "demotion" to second string and I didn't want to waste an opportunity to make the coaches look bad for choosing someone else to start over me, even though I was clearly better.

I was head and shoulders better than my own teammate who was my competitor. I wanted the team and the newspapers to question the coach's decisions, to highlight the politics in a way. I got gratification making the coaches look bad. When I would play, I would make so many more plays than the starter in my position and do it effortlessly. I wasn't even tired. I worked out with intentions to make big plays and highlight the coaching staff's faults. It was my motivation to be faster and play more aggressive. I led the team with tackles and every time we scored that year, it was while I was involved in a play.

Off the field, I was still struggling as well. I acted out and started spiraling out of control without even noticing it happening. In a way, I didn't have guidance. I put so much of my life into controlling my football career and felt I was taking steps backward. I was doing well in school, but mentally breaking down. I had a fake ID and would go out often. I didn't know who I was emotionally or spiritually. I didn't know how to deal with rejection or adversity, which is what I felt from my coaches. I would be diligent Monday through Wednesday but Thursday through Sunday, I was a wild man, drinking, partying, hanging out with random girls and not taking good care of myself. I fought with a lot of people and slept around. My ego was growing, but so did an internal depression. I didn't know what was wrong or how to fix it, but I didn't want to talk to any of my coaches. I hated them all. I felt betrayed and it set a tone of hatred I had for my position coach all through college. I had to deal with the shame of not starting, the feeling of rejection, anger and the politics that followed. I felt I wasn't given a fair shot. I had to operate individually but think collectively for the team.

We were going into the season as the number one preseason team. We were set up to win but never meshed. We had off- field issues. One of our All-American linebackers got a DUI, missed games just to come back and get caught again. We had great potential but no unity or brother-hood. There were people playing that shouldn't have been, the com-munication was all off. Here we had some of the best college football players in the country at the time but we couldn't get it together. That just shows how important morale and correspondence is for a team to be a winning team.

Teams need to have guys strong enough to go to the coaches and explain how things off the field are hurting the team; coaches need to be able to take that and run with it. When you are only focused on winning, it won't work. We lost a lot of big games that year. I took my games and practices as my pre-spring ball prep. I knew I would probably start the following year but knew our 1996 year was one that we each had to push the reset button on, and ask ourselves individually and collectively if we were part of the problem or the solution? What did me showing up the coaches prove? That I was better than them? That they underestimated me? It didn't help our team, or me personally.

I went into the offseason with a drink in my hand. I drank when I was upset but also when it was time to celebrate. Grant Wistrom and Jason Peters both had chances to turn pro early. They announced early in the offseason they were coming back to help the team get to the National Championship again. That was the excitement the team needed to change up the attitude and give us energy. They sacrificed money and their careers to help us, we had to match them from a work ethic and accountability stand point.

We all went out to celebrate and partied hard. I drank Long Island Iced Teas one after another, ten of them I think, only to wake up the next morning totally fine as if I had nothing but water all night. I didn't even remember what had happened the night before, but found out we got kicked out of the bar. It was then that I realized I was creating a problem for myself and if I didn't get my drinking under control, it was going to control me.

I called Coach Young to tell him I felt maybe I had developed a drinking problem. I remember it was the day before the draft and when he should have been helping and assisting players he had getting drafted, he took time out of his schedule to set me up with the team psychologist to get me the help I needed. I remember having mixed emotions, because I felt betrayed by all the coaches the prior year, but here was Coach Osborne taking time to listen to my fears and help me get my life back on track; nothing to do with football. I realized how much he cared about his players and their well-being overall. He set me up with Jack Stark who was the team psychologist to help players with their problems off the field. It was while meeting with him often I found out I didn't have a drinking problem per se, but an adversity problem. I didn't deal with adversity in my life. From when I was a child to a young adult, I didn't have the techniques in place to deal with problems without hurting myself emotionally and physically. I went through counseling with him to get my body and mind right for life and also to get mentally refocused on football. I needed to rebound to make my comeback, if not for anyone else, for myself.

Three things to do when dealing with adversity:

1. Recognize the problem, but don't dwell on it. A lot of people paralyze themselves with what they did wrong when they should never forget what they did but FORGIVE themselves. After forgiveness, clear vision will come.
2. Seek help from a professional. Too many people have an ego issue when it comes to opening up about challenges. Funny thing is, people have tons of advice but seldom take their own.
3. Find an upper classmen or person to try and emulate. Yes, copying is the ultimate sign of flattery but when you are down and out you better set that ego aside and emulate someone who does it right. Why? Because after a while, you will be into a routine that will help you rebound faster and give you confidence if you fall off the wagon in the future.
4. Realize that it doesn't last forever. Torment only lasts as long as you let it. Recognize it, heal and move on.

Six

The Third Ring

During this time of healing, I tried to re-build some relationships in my life. My mom and I had grown apart during high school and early college, as I simply just didn't have time to spend with her and had my own things going on. I was also hardened from things I had "heard." I tried to start making my own decisions about which people were or were not going to be in my life. I started talking to her on a more regular basis. It was a snail's pace, but she was very respectful of me needing space to advance. I was always told she would want something of me, but every time I spoke with her I only left feeling she wanted nothing but my happiness and success. I was passively open to getting to know who she was versus who I was told she was. As much as I enjoyed our conversations, I often times left confused as well.

I started seeing myself in her. She showed me she was able to survive on her own and had great work ethic. She was very focused and competitive as well as a hard worker. I felt that I had some of the same traits. Many people think that I get that from my dad, but really the willingness to do whatever it takes to win is from my mom. She never let me win games growing up; it was a good thing for me. I started gaining confidence after I would talk to her. Having a better relationship with my mom made my life a lot better to say the least.

During this time, I also connected with my sister, Tianna, who oddly enough, lived in Omaha. My dad had always told me about her, but I never met her until I was 17 years old. She was six months younger than me. Yes, my dad was a little bit of a "playa" back then. I knew my dad didn't see her much so I didn't know what she expected from me. I didn't know if I should reach out to her or find her, but I also didn't want to disrespect my dad either if he didn't want to be involved in that way. It is crazy how the mind can bring things to life. Soon after I began wondering about her on a daily basis, she reached out to me through the team and left me a message. I wasn't sure how to proceed and was still very untrusting of people, specifically women, thinking she would want something from me.

She came down to my apartment on a Sunday morning. There were four football players sobering up from practice and hangovers, eating cereal and playing video games when my sister came to meet me for the first time. I was 21 years old and felt like I was having a true adult moment. The feelings I had or were supposed to have, were very unfamiliar. I typically distanced outside things but didn't want to be impolite to her. I took her to lunch and showed her around the campus. Even though I knew she was family, I felt she was a stranger. I kept expecting her to ask me for something, questions about my dad, or tickets to a game, but she never did. She wasn't trying to set herself up for personal gain; she truly just wanted a relationship with her brother. It was an eye-opening experience to finally realize that all women aren't that bad. It was probably perfect timing in that I was more mature and could handle things a little better.

There was a lot of self-discovery during that time in my life. I opened myself up to people and asked a lot of hard questions. I had a skewed perception of women. My mom wasn't around, my dad's girlfriends were back and forth, but here was a girl who genuinely wanted the best for me and just wanted to connect with me as a sibling. I wasn't used to someone who just wanted the best for me without having personal gain in it, but I was starting to find people like that in my life. I enjoyed spending time with my sister and soon we became comfortable being around each other. My dad wasn't super excited that my sister and I were becoming close or that my mom and I were communicating better. Maybe he was concerned about the stories he had told me versus the life I saw them live. Regardless, it wasn't his choice for me anymore. I felt like I was maturing in areas of my life and wanted to see other points of view.

I challenged myself to get my grades as high as I could and applied myself with time management. I became more proud of myself and what I was doing in the classroom than what I was doing on the field. I started to value my learning experience and valuing myself. When my mind was calm and my emotions were stable, I found that my skills excelled to the next level on the field as well.

I was starting in spring ball, and I was a true starter. I didn't have to fight an upper classman to show I belonged. I was now set to get the respect from teammates and coaches. I was set up to be a leader on the team, the middle linebacker, the leader of the defense. It was a big year on and off the field. I was a leader, but being a leader means you are not afraid to ask for help. I had to take care of myself before I could take care of anyone else. I had a lot of self-evaluation and positive vibes going into that season. The year before, I was a train wreck and becoming an alcoholic. I was sleeping with a lot of women and abusing my body, basically trying to hurt myself, which was weird to think about in the natural mind. I heard once that about 60-70% of kids going into college have some sort of mental issue, a vice of sorts, but learning what triggers it and how to control it is key. Some people party too hard or can't handle the academics or turn to drugs. I felt fortunate to get it under control instead of falling into the pitfalls of it. I focused on my health and got my weight to about 235 lbs. I looked like a linebacker and had my mind focused on the right things.

Every minute of my day was accounted for with energy and thoughts to become a better person and football player. I dedicated myself to the weight room and to academics. My mind set was good, the individualism went out of my system, and I felt more a part of the team.

I was motivated that year and loved every moment of putting my name out there and backing it up. One game we played was on the road to the University of Washington. We were doing a walk-through and the official calling the game, Jim Wacker, came and introduced himself. This was the former coach of the University of Minnesota who didn't want to recruit me. When Coach Osborne wasn't around, I walked right up to him and introduced myself, followed with a "FUCK YOU! You didn't want to recruit me. I'm glad you got fired and I'll show you tomorrow why you should have recruited me!"

As much as I was in a good place mentally and emotionally, he pulled the tension and motivation out of me when I saw him. Kindness wasn't in my vocabulary or makeup at the time. Kindness is never compatible with football. A couple of my teammates looked at me shocked. I was shocked too and was scared Coach Osborne would find out. Jim Wacker seemed a bit shocked too but smirked. We were on a national stage and I put him and the nation on notice to know we were back and ready. We had a great game and I know I earned his respect that day.

Later that year we played Missouri. My teammate, Mike Rucker, had an ax to grind with them. That was his hometown and they passed on him as a recruit. We never considered them a rival because we always won but still wanted to hand it to them hard to prove a point. The night before the game, we saw they were watering the field. Immediately we knew they were doing it to try to negate our speed. The next day, the field was so wet, we felt like we were playing in quicksand. We didn't play as well, as we were significantly slower. We were losing when we got the ball with a minute and a half left. Scott Frost caught a pass play, threw it in the end zone, got tipped by a defender and Matt Davis caught it for a touchdown to tie the game for overtime.

We went into overtime and ended up winning with Mike Rucker making the game saving play, propelling us to what would be a National Championship season. The next two games went by in a breeze and we were off to the Big 12 Championship. The same Championship we let go the season before. We were set to play Texas A&M. Needless to say, we didn't need any more motivation, but we got it from an unlikely source. Shortly after knowing what team we were going to play, there were rumors that Coach Osborne was sick and was going to retire. We kept that information in-house and used it as fuel. Very few guys knew but the ones that did kept it under wraps.

We didn't just beat A&M next, we demolished them. We dominated them from the very first series to the last play. We sent those punk Texas boys home with a grade A ass beating. It was a game everyone got their rocks off. It was a great feeling heading into a bowl game. We were now laser focused and in sync with each other, a drastic change from the prior year.

We were set to play Tennessee, against Peyton Manning in the Orange Bowl for the National Championship. It's crazy that I got to play against him considering me and him ran around the Vikings locker room when were young and now he was the golden child of college football. That year, the guys and I were wild and we didn't give a damn who we would piss off or anything else. Upon arriving to the Orange Bowl, we had three nights with no curfew. I thought, "Oh, hell no... they were giving us a free pass after practice and I'm of legal age to get in the bars? Trouble." Like I have always said, we pushed things to the limit, but never over.

The second night we were out, we ran into Trey Teague and Peyton Manning at a bar. I introduced myself and my other teammates and exchanged pleasantries. One thing I did was tell Trey Teague I was going to be knee deep in his ass come the game. We prepared hard and played hard at night. From the girls, the parties and running into NFL players we had a blast, but never lost focus. The week's practice leading up to the game was crisp every day, from meetings to on-field work. I think every guy had the eye of the tiger. The goal was to send T.O. (Tom Osborne) out on a high note because he was retiring after the game.

1994 Orange Bowl in Miami for the National title.
As you can tell we were there to have a good time before the game. Kenny
Cheatham, Trey Crayton, Mike Rucker, Octavius McFarlane, Jamel
Williams, Me, Aaron Davis, Michael Booker and John Livingston.

When we woke up the morning of the game, we all had a feeling something big was about to happen. We walked into the locker room and it seemed like a funeral. No one was hurt or in trouble, but there was that rumor that Coach Osborne was going to retire. Why would he announce it now? We were about the play the National Championship against Peyton Manning's "team of destiny" and this is Coach Osborne's last game? We wanted to win so badly for Coach Osborne. Tennessee was loaded with NFL talent on both sides of the ball, from Al Wilson, to Shawn Bryson, to Cosey Coleman.

It was a close game at first, but we ended up putting everything we had in it, all the problems from the year before and all the work to get in sync with each other that year and stay healthy. We fought hard and beat Tennessee 42-17, giving Coach Osborne his last National Championship

Title for a retirement gift. Little did I know that his retiring would change the university forever.

Tony Ortiz, Eric Johnson, Mike Rucker, Jay Gates and me. Pregame picture with the trophy we knew was ours. We played Peyton Manning and Tennessee for all the marbles. They didn't have a chance because we always prepared with a purpose and had the will to win at all costs.

Seven

LEARNING HOW TO BE A LEADER

I realized after the championship game that I had played well enough to be considered for the NFL Draft as an early entry. It wasn't because of gaudy numbers or anything, but I had accomplished everything I set out to do in college, and I felt I couldn't trust my position coach due to him letting me down the prior year. My dad was talking to scouts trying to weigh the different options. The roster of our team was depleted with the departure of all-time Nebraska greats like Grant Wistrom, Jason Peter, Aaron Taylor, Scott Frost, Eric Warfield and Ahman Green. With the seniors leaving and Coach Osborne retiring it was a different feeling, a bit of uneasy ground, but I felt I had an obligation to Nebraska to give them one more year. I loved Nebraska, the university, our team, Coach Solich and Coach McBride. I would never turn my back on any of them for my own personal gain.

When I look back, I wish I would have reconsidered because of the lack of depth of the linebackers in the draft that year. Hindsight is 20/20 and in this case it would have worked in my favor. But in the grand scheme of things, I think the experience of being a captain and that year of transition really helped me when I went to the next level. I think I had a crash course on chaos that year.

Based solely on my own personal experience, my thoughts on Coach Solich are that he is a good man and a great coach. One thing about Coach Solich that I will always respect is that he expected your best and when things got tough, he expected you to "figure it out." He was upfront and honest with me, and I will never forget that. Some players called him "Fastball Frank" for whatever reason, but with me, I felt if you earned his respect, he would go to bat for you in every way possible. He was thrust into a hard situation. He came under some heat after I left, but I will say he didn't get a fair shake when it came to getting another year to get it right. I will tell you this, when I called Frank later in life about coaching, he was the only one that had a spot for me. I regret not taking that job, but I had personal issues to take care of and didn't want to leave my kids. Coach Solich was the type of guy who, anytime I called him, would call me back right away. He was still loyal to me after I was out of the program. To sum it up, he's my guy.

**Coach Solich and me on Senior Day. Time went too fast.
I have nothing but respect for this man.**

I wanted to step up my game and be part of a new era. There were about twenty-five of us going into our senior year and a lot was expected of us for the team. Even with all the guys that left, the expectations never would change. We had been in this position before when Tommie Frazier left. I was selected to be on the unity council that year and was happy to be in a leadership position. There was one kid on the team named Brandon. He was a defensive lineman so I knew I needed to depend on him. He worked hard and was strong. I thought he was a good kid. I knew he could develop into a great player over time. I found myself checking on him often, getting on a more personal level with him. I tended to draw to the player that worked hard and sacrificed to win and that's who he was. I saw a lot of myself in him when it came to that. It didn't matter to me if he was black, white, from the country or the city. My love for my teammates had no preference.

One weekend he went to the club and had way too many drinks. One thing led to another and after hitting on the bouncer's girlfriend and getting into an altercation, my man called the bouncer (who happened to be black) every racial slur known to man and even some I hadn't heard before. Any other time, it would have been a case of his word against mine type of thing, but there was video and audio that was turned over to the coaches. One thing about Lincoln is word travels fast and soon the accounts of the night were all the same from various sources. The unity council and coaches had to meet to review the tape to decide if he was going to get kicked off the team. He came in and apologized, said he had gotten out of control and was going to lay off the alcohol for a while. I wanted to give him another chance, he was my friend, but then I started to wonder if he really was my friend if this was the way he was talking.

It was a hard decision but we couldn't keep him on the team. It was a decision I still think about to this day. What made a decision like that hard was that it could affect him for the rest of his life. Maybe he had aspirations for the NFL or always wanted to play at Nebraska. Our country believes in second chances, right? I think it was weighed if he would help the team or not and what he may have done in the past.

I remember him calling me and pleading with me to help him, crying on the other line. I couldn't do anything for him. Every time I saw him, he would apologize and I would accept it. I felt horrible though; my leadership role was tough as I was crushing a guy's dream based off one incident. Brandon went on to get married and enlist in the Navy, but we never talked too much after that. The value of the lesson was great for me. Even now in my personal life and in corporate America, I find that I still reflect on that decision with Brandon when evaluating employees and doing what's best overall for the company. I am not a super emotional type of guy, but learning how to make these types of decisions was hard, yet had to be done. We needed our team to be strong even though it was evident early on in the season we weren't going to be as good as the year before.

My senior year went by faster than I expected. I wanted to go out on top like some of the other classes, but this was a "transition" year. If there ever was a year not to be a senior, this was it. I think we held our own defensively, but we were out of sync offensively with players and coaches. Our biggest weakness was not having a quarterback who was truly ready to step in. Frankie London was the veteran and played behind Scott Frost, but it seemed like no matter what, they weren't going to start Frankie. This was the year of Bobby Newcombe and Eric Crouch.

Bobby had made a name for himself as a punt returner and wing back in his short time. He was a quarterback in high school and they had visions of him being the next Tommie Frazier. There was only one Tommie Frazier. There weren't any similarities except they were both black. Crouch, on the other hand, had the intangibles and toughness needed to play, but he was too skinny, according to the coaches. I remember him being frustrated and wanted to quit and go home. I told him to stick it out and his time would come. Eric eventually went on to win the Heisman Trophy, the highest honor in college football. The best thing about Eric is that he's a down to earth dude and you would never know he was a stud if you saw him on the street.

Personally, my senior year went great. I was a semi-finalist for the Butkus Award (given to the top linebacker in college) and was All Big-12. With that being said, I still felt empty because we lost four games that season. It was viewed as a failure by our standards. The game I think of when I think of that season, is the home loss to Texas. We hated Texas ever since the formation of the Big-12, but they seemed to have our number. They had the eventual Heisman winner, Ricky Williams. Ricky had a NCAA record for consecutive games with a touchdown. We were the only defense to hold him without a touchdown. To me, it was whip cream on horseshit!!

I made a pact to myself that no matter what, if I made it to the NFL, I was going to try and royally kick every Texas player's ass. We had them by the balls but let them off the hook. We gave up a fifty-yard bomb on third down and twenty-six. Still to this day, I'm pissed about it. We had a NCAA record for consecutive home wins at forty-seven that Texas broke on a Halloween night. In my opinion, I was a part of the beginning of the end of the dominance of Nebraska football. I will say that I saw a big difference in the underclassmen, they were more about themselves and selfish. It was the first of the entitled classes that have ruined our teams for years after I left.

As my college football career was ending, I spent much time reflecting on what it took to play ball on that level. Many people have since asked me advice or thoughts on how to make it in college. I found that being seen and not heard far outweighed the opposite in terms of success. Going into college, you have a lot to prove, whether you were a top recruit or a walk on. Prove it on the field, not with your mouth. Give people something to talk about. I also found that it's not a bad thing to be a copycat. It may sound corny, but by choosing an older player that has it figured out and copy what he did on the field and in practice really helped my game improve to a level of greatness.

Another thing I realized was that sacrifices are necessary. My time and my body was property of the University of Nebraska. There were so many things I missed or didn't partake in because I needed to use the time to focus more on my game. The last thing I realized, that really affected my time in Nebraska, was the importance of managing my personal life. Cutting down the list of friends and investing in yourself and teammates is the best sense of time and overall emotional well-being for a college ball player. I knew as I sat reflecting on these habits I picked up, that they would be able to help take me into the next course of action with the NFL, but there were other main components that I knew would be different.

I had to switch mindsets from focusing mainly on the team that season to realizing this was the last opportunity to propel myself into the next level of football. Although we were losing most of our games, I still played strong and hard to the end of the season. Before the bowl game, agents started calling frequently. The whole agent thing was new to me and I really didn't understand it. I was being offered large amounts of money, cars, and gifts to sign with different agents. I didn't take any of it, feeling it was a trap.

As soon as you stop playing college ball, it turns to straight business. Immediately you start to focus on trying to see if you have a shot to make it to the next level. One of the ways to measure yourself is the all-star games. I was fortunate enough to get an invite to the East/West Shrine game, but wanted to go to the Senior Bowl, which was thought of as the place where all the top prospects were invited. On a side note, I wanted to go because my dad not only went to the Senior Bowl, he won the MVP of the game. Like I said before, it's hard to follow in those footsteps. Along with all-star games comes the agents and runners. They will try anything from giving you cash, chicks, cars and above all else, false promises. One agent I really liked out of Chicago who used to represent Brian Cox, told me I had a special invite to the game and they were making up my jersey and such. Funny thing is I knew it was a lie and far-fetched but played along just for the comedy. He wanted me to sign with him based on his promise and story. When it fell through, he said they took some linebacker from Iowa instead of me. That was the only truth in his story, that there was a linebacker from Iowa there. He tried to say they took him because he was 6'3 and I was 6'1. Well hell, I didn't know the Senior Bowl was like a chick with expectations in the bed, LOL. Regardless, I watched every player at the Senior Bowl, watched their film, read their stats and compared them to mine as much as someone possibly could.

When I went to the East/West Shrine game, I was under the radar. I practiced hard and went against great players who I watched in college like Jon Jansen. Jon went on to play for over ten years in the NFL for the Redskins and Detroit. After a few hard days, I was starting to get noticed which was great but the hard part was I hadn't picked an agent by then. I felt the pressure and wanted to have a big name agent, thinking he would work harder for me. The myth is that a bigger agent or agency can or would do more, that's false. Agents or agencies are who they are regardless of how many clients they have or not. Oddly enough, my roommate, Mike Rucker, was ranked high for the NFL draft, highly recruited and ended up being drafted in the second round by the Carolina Panthers. His agent was Peter Schaffer. I first met Pete at the East/West game and we hit it off. One thing I liked was his image and his work ethic. His hardest battle was selling my dad, and I don't think he ever could do so. My dad liked a smaller agent out of Denver, Colorado that had recruited me longer than Pete had. My young and dumb mindset didn't think he was big time enough, and I was tired of my dad trying to control my sports career so ended up signing with Peter Schaffer. I may have done so out of spite or rebellion, but either way, I was on my way or so I thought. I later found out that promises had been made to the other agent that I didn't know about. I didn't like that because it made me look like a fool, but one thing Peter said was that in his business he had seen or heard it all. This was my first experience with the part of the NFL that is dealt with outside of the white lines. I often wonder if this happened with a lot of players or was it just in extreme cases. Word of your personal life and people around you travel fast in the NFL regardless if it is right or wrong. One thing the league will do is try and label or pin you into a stereotype before you ever lace up some cleats. Life isn't fair, right?

To be successful in football, business, life, or anything for that matter, you have to have a good team and foundation around you. With my dad being involved, I sometimes felt like I wanted to do just the opposite, because I wanted to show him I could survive on my own. Regardless if he was right or wrong about who I chose to have represent me, it was true that he didn't go about it the right way.

Always remember the agent works for you and you don't work for him.

To have the best chance in making it, a player needs a good foundation, a good mentor, brutally honest friends, a good agent, and an excellent trainer. Everyone has to be on the "Jay Foreman" train, per se. If one of them isn't with you 100% they need to go and don't look back. One thing that is hard for some parents is that they sometimes relive their lives through their kids. If not handled right it could be a detriment to your career. I knew early in my football life that I most likely wasn't going to reach the heights my dad had reached, and to be honest, I was okay with that. I understood from my time at Nebraska that there are more factors than I could name into who is pushed to be assumed the best or better players.

The one thing I wish I could get through the minds of young athletes is that you never know who you can trust until you say no or you are broke. Funny part about sports is sometimes your family and friends think they get paid on your pay day just like you. Sometimes they act and plan their life in a way expecting you to be their safety net. I can remember people needing new fences, cars, money and whatever else they thought was needed to make their life easier. Again, who works for who? I think Lebron James did it and does it best. He brought all his closest friends along, got them educated and taught them business. Now they are building on their own along with him. Two answers to learn are "NO" and "FUCK YOU." The latter you will need when people get upset when you tell them NO. Trust me!

A few things to look for when choosing an agent:

1. Look for anyone that you know or have a connection to that they have represented. It's a fact that the best way to get the real deal about an agent is to talk to other players. They typically won't lie to you.

2. Look at the size of class he has during your draft year. An agent or agency can only service so many guys. You want who recruited you to be the one who does your deal. Make sure your agent doesn't try to push you off onto an intern or someone like that. Some agents get lazy after you sign with them.

3. Negotiate your own percentage you feel you want to pay your agent. My advice is between 1-2%. Standard percentage is 3%, but most contracts are slotted and therefore agents don't really have to do much.

4. DO NOT LET THE AGENT CONTROL YOUR FINANCES IN ANY WAY! I think that is self- explanatory.

5. Make sure all training, food and travel are taken care of by your agent. A good agent will line you up to be trained before the combine and the draft. They should never charge you back for that. If they try and charge you back, that lets you know they are shady and don't believe in you.

6. Keep your family and your agent away from one another. Too many agents get into your circle and it makes it hard to fire him if they aren't working.

7. Keep your financial advisor and agent separate. Do not have someone that is connected to your agent do your finances. When

an agent knows all your business, he has the advantage. They will negotiate with your personal info in mind. Bad move!

8. Don't be scared to fire them. If you feel they aren't getting the job done, fire them. Best believe, if you aren't getting picked up or making them money, they will do the same.

Eight

Meat Market – The NFL Combine

Peter was very good about helping me get focused for the combine. He was upfront with me about several great linebackers coming to the draft and said I would be a third to fifth round draft pick. When the combine rolled around, I felt confident. I had an agent, and I had been training extensively for three to four weeks. I knew I was going to test well. I was prepared for the testing but not for the gawking.

The combine is a unique experience. I considered it similar to being a woman who is getting cat called or stared at in the club constantly. We were lined up like cattle, shuffling along to the different rooms and stations, each having their own level of importance. They check everything, your calf size to your quad size. They even look at the skin tone and compare it to your stats. The darker players were more feared since they were perceived to be more aggressive, the lighter skin tone was thought to be softer.

We were led one by one to the auditorium where 300-500 people sat in the audience. Our weight and name were on the big screen as we walked on the stage individually in our underwear. We couldn't see anyone in the crowd, just the high velocity lights streaming down on our bodies. I was instructed to stand still facing front, then turn to the side, to the back and the other side for pictures. As I posed, all I heard was the feverish speed of pens clicking to write notes in the audience. It was very intimidating and awkward. People were drawing opinions based solely on their personal perception. No one can prepare you for that cattle call. I felt like a new slab of meat on display. I've heard people compare the combine to slave trade, I can see what they mean or get that idea. The idea of that thought is on point but obviously it's in a certain context. Point is that you are always a number and just depends on what number you are to start with.

After the auditorium experience, we met with the scouts for interviews. There were thirty-one teams to interview with and the scouts or interns would grab you for ten to fifteen minutes each. They tried to get a feel for you the best they could during that time. I grew up around some of the scouts so I felt pretty comfortable in that situation, way more than the previous one. I focused on a good interview and running a good forty. You never really know what they are looking for, athletically or personality wise. I was still a kid with an alpha male attitude and had no problem putting that on display, because I knew I had the skills to back it up.

While talking to Tennessee, the linebacker coach asked me the same question five times, "If you were a rookie and there was a vet who wasn't earning his keep, being lazy or not practicing, what would you do?" I told him I would expect the leader of the team to say something, but if I was playing well enough I would say something. He followed up with, "You wouldn't be scared of a vet? How tough are you?" This quickly prompted me to challenge him to come find out. Most young coaches try and test you and push your buttons. Funny part is that I was interviewing those teams just as much as they were interviewing me.

The one general manager I remember is Bill Polian. He was the mastermind who helped the Buffalo Bills experience four straight Super Bowls, then went to the Carolina Panthers and made them into a team to be reckoned with. He was straight forward and brash. I think he tried to test players to see if they were mentally weak or strong. He did so by dressing down each player to the point they might question themselves. At first he was a turn off, but I soon realized he'd most likely shoot it to you straight if you ever spoke to him in private. Honesty comes few and far between in the NFL business. As you go along your career you know who's a good general manager or not and Mr. Polian is one of the best and is in the Hall of Fame.

At the NFL Combine, you meet plenty of players from big schools and small that all have the same dream. Two that I remember most were Joey Porter and Keith Newman. Both guys were in my group when we tested. What I remember about Joey is that we always seemed to look and see what each other did, but we never really spoke. I guess we had the macho thing going on to not let anyone else think they are better. Joey beat me in the vertical jump when he jumped thirty-nine inches. Funny fact about Joey is that he was a wide receiver for Colorado State his first few years before switching over to defense. Pittsburgh drafted him and he quickly became one of their best linebackers of all time. In my opinion, he has a chance for the NFL Hall of Fame.

The other guy was Keith Newman. I knew about Keith from various magazines and scouting reports. Those reports didn't do him any justice. He was huge and could move. He looked forty years old when he was only twenty-two, never changing his facial expressions. People thought he was always angry, but he was cool with me. He had a chip on his shoulder just like me and we bonded over proving people wrong. Keith was a part of the UNC pipeline of players to the NFL from their defenses.

Overall, I did well. Coaches were shocked with my common sense and football intelligence. I had a Plan A, Plan B, and a Plan C and buying their bullshit wasn't a part of any of the plans. I realized however, that even with all the talking, I knew the next day I would have to really show my speed and strength for testing.

When it was time to run the forty, several guys said they had injuries and couldn't run. There were still enough guys that were going for me to compete with to show my speed. My first run was 4.68. I wasn't happy with the time and got myself pissed off knowing I would run better if angry. The next one I ran was 4.58 and then 4.63. With that last run, I had the fastest linebacker time that ran that day and had a great chance to be drafted. Back then your draft life depended on your forty yard dash time and bench press numbers, both of which mean nothing when you have pads on. I remember talking to Peter and him telling me what times and numbers I needed to hit based on what guys did before. I learned the main thing you want to do is test well enough to not only validate your game tape but also jump out to where the scouts have to go back and look even closer. The worst thing you can do is either show up unprepared or scared. Some guys can't handle that pressure of "running for a check." The base times I needed to hit were 4.7 or faster in the forty and twenty reps or above in the bench. I passed both easily. I will say that Jeven Kearse or Mike Peterson (both guys from Florida Gators) didn't run but I still did what I needed to do to get noticed.

Nine

LIFE LONG DREAM

The NFL Draft is a weird thing. It's not necessarily the best player who rises to the top, but more like whoever a specific team is looking for: a certain height, a certain weight, or a backup player for an aging starter. It had me all confused. I was trying to be realistic about the process, knowing I would be anywhere from a late second round pick to a free agent. I flew to DC with my family. I didn't want a big party. I wanted to watch and let my agent do what he was supposed to do. He was a lawyer and grinded but was stressed when he would talk to me because my dad was so overbearing.

The whole house was full of tension on draft day. I played on one of the best teams in the history of college football, and I knew my test scores and my production. I did all I could to get to this point and it was time to see if I would go on. I felt a lot of pressure and I prepared myself mentally to get let down a bit, and to have to go out and prove to them I was worth the shot, something I had done before. Before I knew it, the third round ended and they would resume the following day. I didn't sleep at all. I knew if it was going to happen it would be the following day. I had a good feeling and started getting calls. In the fourth round, Dallas called, then Cleveland, followed by Carolina. I had great interviews with both of those teams and was optimistic.

Carolina drafted my roommate in the second round, so I was hopeful I would go there with him. The linebacker coach told me I was at the top of their list. My time was now, so I thought! The draft is a funny thing, because it rarely goes the way you hope. The big news that year was that the New Orleans Saints gave up the farm for Ricky Williams. Although Ricky was good, it seemed far-fetched to mortgage your whole team for one player. To the Saints' credit, they had some dawgs on defense and Coach Mike Ditka was always a run and grind it out kind of coach. Some say that a trade like that messed up everyone's draft board, and there becomes a position that falls. Some said it would be linebackers. I personally thought it was bullshit, but you believe anything when you are hoping to get drafted.

In the fourth round, Cleveland was up and set to pick a linebacker, I thought for sure this would be it for me because I had a great workout with them. Unfortunately, they ended up picking Wali Ranier, a guy I played against in the East/West Shrine game. I was disappointed and cussed them out under my breath and stormed out of the house to get some fresh air. One sliver of hope was that the Panthers were picking next. My agent had a good feeling about them because they had just picked my roommate in the second round and they also had drafted a few Nebraska players I played with in college. The night before the second day of the draft the Panthers linebacker coach and scout both called me and said they were really interested in picking me. I thought if there was any place I wanted to go it would be there because it would be just like college and me and the other guys would be the foundation of the Panthers. We were steadily watching the screen when they ended up picking Hannibal Navies from Colorado. They wanted a guy they could develop to come off the edge. He ended up having a good career and we played one season together in San Francisco. After that pick I felt like the world was over.

In the fifth round, the Vikings were up and still needed a linebacker, but I knew the coach probably didn't want my dad around much because the coach at the time only wanted any outside attention on him. I grew up a Vikings fan and who wouldn't want to play for their home town team? To top it off, I felt like there was some ill will or beef from the Vikings towards my dad. It seemed crazy because he was one of their best players of all time. Maybe it was because my dad always spoke his mind and didn't kiss ass. Rumor has it that there is a prominent person in the organization who is trying to keep my dad out of the NFL Hall of Fame. I would like to think the draft is solely based off of who is the best in the position needed, but sometimes film is the last thing a coach may look at. There are politics and favors involved as well. I wasn't surprised when they passed me right by and chose Chris Jones from Clemson. One of the best linebackers in Vikings history and the Denny Green era was Eddie McDaniel. Eddie was small but a good player from Clemson. I guess they felt they were getting Eddie Mac part two. I will say, it didn't work out that way.

I was devastated and pissed off. I took the remote and threw it against my grandma's wall. She quickly reprimanded me and told me to sit down, only to come hug me and tell me to put this feeling on the field when I get a team. By this time, I wasn't even picky anymore. I just knew I didn't want to go to Green Bay or Buffalo, who were the two teams that didn't interview me and I thought there would probably be nothing fun about living in those areas. Funny how as a kid you would die to play on the moon as long as it's the NFL, but all of a sudden you want to pick your team based on night life. How stupid is that? Young mind I tell ya!

While sitting in the living room feeling the strain of my future, the phone rang. It was a 716 area code. I sat there looking at the phone, wondering where the hell 716 area code was when my uncle loudly bolted from his chair and said, "Boy, answer the damn phone!!"

I quickly picked up the phone and heard, "Jay Foreman? This is John Butler from the Buffalo Bills. We didn't think you would still be waiting for a call but we want to draft you!" Chills went through my body as a sigh of relief exited. He asked, "Do you want to be a Buffalo Bill?" I was so relieved and elated that I yelled, "F*** YEAH!! Oh, sorry Coach…yes I would, and thank you!" He didn't skip a beat when he said, "We are going to draft you next. You can earn it and do special teams."

My girlfriend was sitting next to me and could hear the conversation. She quickly got my family together to wait for me to get off the phone to see what was happening. I started talking to different coaches as my name flashed across the bottom of the screen, *Jay Foreman, 5th round draft pick to the Buffalo Bills.* My family erupted with cheers, hugging and congratulating me. The hostility left the room and we had a party to celebrate. It was a great feeling to accomplish such an esteemed goal.

Draft Day - A lot of emotions going on inside me and my family. A minute before this I was cussing the whole world out because I hadn't been picked yet but when the Buffalo Bills called it was the happiest day of my life. Blessed.

My dad was happy I was going to Buffalo. It was a winning team with a winning organization. In 1999, I would soon embark on a journey that would be fun, challenging, frustrating, enjoyable, fruitful, and down-right dirty. As I look back, I find it funny that one of the two places I didn't want to go ended up being the best starting place for my career. I remember thinking to myself, "…all I want is to get drafted and last four years and I'd be happy." Now that I was drafted I wanted more, but I would have to be patient. That isn't my best quality.

Ten

JUST ANOTHER ROOKIE

Rookie mini-camp was about a week or two after the draft. I was excited to get there and prove myself once again to the coaching staff and other players. Right after the draft your mind switches to football mode, which is good. As happy as I was to get drafted, I knew I was going to start at the bottom and nothing was going to be given to me. In the NFL, when you are a fifth round pick you have to earn and take everything you get. Buffalo sent a workout package and itinerary for travel for the next weeks; the NFL was soon to be a reality.

I flew to Chicago and from there took a small plane to Buffalo. As we landed, the pilot came across the speaker to welcome us to Buffalo. I was so pumped for this new adventure. In my excitement, I rolled up the window to look outside and was shocked. It was the beginning of May and there was still snow on the ground. It was rainy and overcast. There was an old rusty barn at the end of the runway that had a faded "Welcome to Buffalo" sign. I felt like I was in *Rocky 4* when he flew into Russia to train. My old and new teammate Sheldon Jackson, who was also drafted to Buffalo, looked at me and we started laughing. We definitely weren't in Kansas (or Nebraska) anymore.

We got our luggage and "Money Mike," the team liaison picked us up. He had about eight of us in the car. I casually hopped in the front seat and optimistically asked him where we were going. He grinned and said he was taking us to the team doctor for a physical. I don't like doctors much so I needed clarification, "Are we getting a shot or checking our blood pressure or something?" He laughed and said, "Yep, and something else... you have to get checked for a hernia, and he'll check your prostate." I had no idea what he was talking about, but started feeling uncomfortable with the sound of that. I asked, "What does that mean?" Mike wasted no time in turning the music down and telling us, "You have to have a full physical, the doctor has to stick his finger in your butt... we call him Dr. Long-finger."

I suddenly went pale. The mood of the van changed and everyone was quietly looking at each other. Mike was laughing at all the rookies sweating it out in the car. When we got to the doctor's office, we decided who would go first. We all waited in the car until it was our turn. I was second. I still remember the face of the guy who went in first coming back to the car. I was so traumatized by that physical and whole experience. Mike was laughing so hard as we walked back to the car. He was all but crying from his laughter. I'm not sure, but I think a couple guys had a tear in their eye when they got back to the car. When we were all done and Mike was trying to gain his composure, I spoke up and said, "Listen man, what else do we have to do? Tell me now before we go any further." I called my dad and he laughed and said it couldn't get any worse.

We went to our dorms and got settled, checked out the facilities, had meetings, then met on the field. It was unnerving at first because we were going from a controlled setting knowing the guys we were going against in college to playing with the best of the best. Even though I was drafted, that didn't mean I would make the final roster. I heard how brutal cuts were and I had to make sure to perform at 100% every practice to secure my spot.

My college teammate, Sheldon Jackson, was a tight end and I was a linebacker, if it came down to him and me, I knew I had to take him out.

It was business. That's the big difference between college and pro, you have to be cut-throat. There are no friends because everyone is playing for a check. My agent always told me "Don't get close to anyone because you never know when they'll be cut." That can be emotional if you are invested emotionally into another player like you were in college.

There was a little bit of harmless rookie hazing. I went to get some practice uniforms and all the shorts that were being handed out to the rookies were these grey daisy-duke style shorts. We all looked like John Stockton, but it was part of the experience. We were rookies. My dad had told me beforehand to make sure I got in good with the equipment guy. I did that right away and he made sure I got the better uniform a few days later.

Rookie mini-camp was a totally different workout. It was a reality check to take my practice to the next level. I took my learning experience serious, even down to the diet. They would give us eggbeaters to lean us out and get rid of any extra body fat we came into camp with. Some guys couldn't handle it.

**Rookie year kicking it in Buffalo with these friends for life.
L to R: Me, Sean Bryson, Brian, and Keith Newman**

I ended up being roommates with Keith Newman, who was also drafted to Buffalo. We called him "Angry Man." He always looked angry, but was totally chill. He was a big, fast, physical dude at 6"4, 245 pounds and 5% body fat. He didn't mess around, he went to bed early, and woke up early. He was all football 100% of the time. The one thing about Keith was that he didn't care what anyone thought or said. He was going to be Keith. He was a great motivator though. He knew the playbook inside and out, so I needed to know it too. He challenged me to play faster. In mini-camp, we would break the huddle and go over plays. We were pulling for each other.

Another guy I clicked with right away was Sean Bryson. We met in the elevator and just matched each other's personality. The first thing he asked me was, "Hey man, do you like white chicks?" I started laughing and responded, "I pride myself on being a man of many nations and do not discriminate." He was from Franklin, North Carolina, a country town that had one stop light. I knew Shawn was for real though because he was a starting running back on the Tennessee squad we beat for the championship. Sean was country fast. Country fast means that he didn't have track form, but he had a stride like a cheetah. He was a good player and an even better dude. Oddly enough, Shawn and I are still best friends and I consider him family.

The other guy I became close with was Keion Carpenter. Keion was a standout safety at Virginia Tech, a school similar to Nebraska. They had a great coach named Frank Beemer and he prided himself on special teams just like Coach Osborne. Right away I knew Keion could play and I could go to war with him. To make things even better was the fact that Keion was from Baltimore, my family was from Frederick, Maryland, so we had that connection. The last thing that brought us close was that we had played against each other in basketball growing up. Crazy how sports can make life come full circle.   That relationship became a lifetime bond. Keion has a great soul and is always there for others. I have never met a person like him before. To top it off, he always had his swag going at 1000. That dude pissed confidence, put confidence in others, and is a natural born leader.

Keion and I shortly before his tragic unexpected death. He was one of the best players I played with and an even better person. He taught me a lot in our little time together but I will never forget him.

A few of the veterans took us out in the evenings to grab a beer. They were very accepting and cool dudes. They really looked out for the younger guys and treated us as equals except when it came time to do the rookie duties. As a rookie, you can expect to carry the vets' pads or sing to them in the dining hall. The main duty was after every game to bring pizza and wings for them to eat or fried chicken on the plane for road trips. On road trips, I tried to get on the plane early to make sure everything was set up for the guys, which made trips easier for all of us. Before one flight, I must have gotten there too early. I went to the restroom after setting up and to my surprise, I ran into a trainer who had a flight attendant bent over the sink giving her the business. I shut the door and went to my seat. He came by a few minutes later and said, "You won't tell anyone what you saw right?" I replied, "What are you talking about? I just got on the plane." The easy way to let people know you are down is to not even acknowledge it. The best part of the whole season was I got out of singing. It wasn't a big deal but I hated getting up in front of people as it was, so singing would have probably given me nightmares. Funny how time changes things because now I do a lot of public speaking.

As training camp got closer, I kept wondering about cuts and if I would be. My position coach in college told me he didn't think I was good enough for the league, so those thoughts came back to me, but I let them drive me. I let that frustration morph me into a better player. I developed a quiet confidence as I continually started beating my own times and runs from college. My agent told me that every day I had to take the personality of a hockey player and fight. I think Peter was right when saying that, but he always wanted to be one of the guys. Scouts told my agent they were thrown off by my quiet demeanor thinking that light skinned players are softer. Yes, you read correctly. Scouts even think skin color matters. They aren't the brightest crayons in the box, but they have to think of things in order to separate players in a predominately black league. Either way, I was working hard to prove that, on the field, I was just as hard and just as tough as anyone else out there. The hardest thing to do as a player is to beat the perception the league has of you. Very rarely can a player do it, but it's a constant battle for most. After all, they do place an expiration date on you like you are a gallon of milk, except it's in years or seasons not days.

I talked to my uncle Butch often and he kept me focused. He was hard on me but pushed me to the max mentally. He told me when camp started, "Whether it's the lineman, fullback, tight- end or running back, bring the dog out of you and earn it."

I was as ready as I was going to be for training camp. I had doubts, but also had skills that I knew were good enough. Right away, the veterans wanted to see what the rookies could do. The number one offense would go against the number two defense. I was going to be back-up for Sam Cowart. He'd had a great season but was injured so he couldn't practice for the first couple weeks. He was cocky, but believed in himself so much he didn't have any problems coaching me. I had to run with the number one defense.

I went to line up and remembered that my uncle had told me that the first play of training camp is usually a run play. There in front of me was Ruben Brown, a big ass running back. "Oh shit!" was all I could say when I saw him. I lined up in front of him and instantly let my intimidation go and wanted to play ball. When the ball snapped, I ran in there and back-doored Ruben. He missed me. I got up talking shit, dancing around. My buddy Sheldon started laughing, as that was the Jay he remembered. That reassured me that I knew I could play. I went on to make mistakes but learned how to correct them. I knew I could play Sam's position and mine. I had what it took to play at this level. The best advice I got as a rookie came from defensive coordinator, Ted Cottrell, who said to learn all four linebacker positions. He told me the more I could do, the safer I would be on the roster. I never forgot that, it helped me in the real world after football as well.

My rookie year out kicking it with my mentor Sam Cowart. He showed me the ropes and taught me the game. If not for injury, I think he would have made the Hall of Fame.

The NFL preseason is heaven and hell mixed into one. It's heaven because you get four games in the NFL but hell in the sense you never know when that will be your last play or game as a football player. One of the things you never get used to is cut days. You see some of the guys you either came in with or drafted with get shipped off to who knows where and you might not hear from them again. When you see someone get cut who you know or watched play before, it takes a little bit out of you. You can try to be hard and not notice it, but for the next two days or so, that's all the guys talk about. Some guys get the short end of the stick, some suck and then some get cut solely due to money. NFL general managers love finding cheap rookies to combine together to replace one veteran. It's the money ball aspect of the NFL, but it rarely works out to be honest. The only time the outcome of the games really doesn't matter is in the preseason. All the players really want is an opportunity to keep their spot and get those checks come the first of the season.

> *Side note: During the preseason, all players are paid the same amount. That's the only time a rookie makes as much as a starting quarterback. I was fortunate enough to have a good enough preseason to make the team, but getting on the game day roster was a whole different animal I had to tackle.*

Eleven

LEARNING THE ROPES

I knew my first year in the NFL I wouldn't get a lot of playing time. I focused on lifting harder and longer and practicing as much as I could. I was inactive on the roster, but worked hard to get a spot during the middle of the season when injuries began to occur. Most rookies don't realize that the film you put out there in the pre-season is a huge deciding factor into whether you are called to play or not.

The first NFL game I played was against Seattle. I was on special teams and was only getting eight to ten plays, but I tried to stay as focused and alert as I could. In my first NFL play, Raion Hill (aka Shitty Ray) and I were instructed to hit between two guys of the three-man wedge and blow up the wedge. It was time to earn my check and my respect. I was ready, the play started and I was running just like we practiced and the wedge was forming. I checked my peripheral and was hauling ass. I looked at Raion and saw he was there as the wedge was coming. For whatever reason, Raion tripped (one of many reasons we call him "Shitty Ray"). I went into the wedge and all four guys converged. Two guys hit me in the head and I was knocked out on site. It felt like slow-motion as I was falling face first onto the Seattle AstroTurf.

I came to when I hit the ground and was struggling a bit. I arose dis-oriented and went running to the wrong sideline.   The referee turned me around and sent me to the right side. I was hurting but had to play it off as if I was laughing about it. It almost felt like a term of endearment to get your first concussion. The trainers broke open the smelling salts and asked if I knew where I was. I heard the announcer over the speaker say, "First down Seattle." I quickly answered and was allowed to play the rest of the game. The days after were harsh and the most difficult re-covery time of my career. It was by far the worst headache I ever had for three weeks.

I ended up playing on special teams the whole season and filled-in for Sam Cowart when he was injured. I proved that I was good on spe-cial teams. I was a reliable back up and could be a starter my first year, realizing it's not necessarily where you start, but where you end that's important. We ended the season 11-5 and I had racked up close to sixty tackles with fourteen special team tackles. The only downer of my first season was the playoff loss to the Tennessee Titans, called the "Music City Miracle." Regardless of any camera angle, THAT WAS A FORWARD PASS. I cringe every time I see that replay on ESPN or some network.

Playoff football is at a whole different speed and intensity. Only the strong survive. I witnessed two starting players fighting at halftime when we had the lead. The fight was short-lived as one of linebackers folded our Hall of Fame defender up into the locker. A Hall of Famer got fold-ed up! Tennessee had a magical year, but we matched up well against them. They were mainly a running team with Eddie George and we were number one in the league against the run. What made this game even harder was that the owner of the team, Ralph Wilson, decided that he wanted Rob Johnson to start over fan favorite and pro-bowl quarterback, Doug Flutie. This caused a big media storm in our locker room and took all of our momentum away heading down to a hornet's nest of an atmo-sphere in Nashville.

Long story short, Rob was knocked out of the game and good ole Flutie flakes came in and led us down to take the lead with a little less than fifteen seconds left. The game should have been over, but all hell broke loose. The coaches decided to squib kick it instead of kicking deep to offset their return chances. By squib kicking it, we gave them the perfect chance to set up their once in a lifetime play to win the game. They ran everyone to one side, kept a few back on the other side, and threw what was a forward pass (later called a lateral) to Kevin Dyson. He ran down the sidelines and scored. Just like that the game and our Super Bowl chances were over. As I watched him run down the sidelines, I saw my extra playoff check going down with every yard he gained until he hit the end zone, and my check was gone. The crowd went crazy. I had never been in a stadium that loud, ever.

To make things worse, I had to go face to face with a Titan's wide receiver, who I had told there was a rumor going around that he was gay. He got mad and shoved me on the sidelines. I was already pissed off after the loss and he had the nerve to come ask me why I said it. I retorted, "Because if it wasn't true you wouldn't have dropped all those passes or be mad." Typical rookie, running my mouth and not thinking about the consequences. He said something back which led to a couple blows being thrown in the tunnel and security breaking it up. Needless to say, I survived and still went out on the town after we landed back in Buffalo. Nature boy style was always in effect after a win or loss.

Off the field, I was trying to find my stride. I went out with the team often and got to experience the groupie mentality of several women. At the time, I didn't really have a lot of experience with the NFL life, so I just thought that was normal. Now, being a married man and a father of girls, I realize how sad it was that women devalue themselves for a title, always chasing a wallet.

I was lonely my rookie year. There wasn't much to do in Buffalo as far as nightlife. I was ready for a change of scenery and called my cousin to come to Buffalo to help me move to Minnesota for the offseason where I had just bought my first bachelor pad. I picked him up from the airport in a snowstorm. My SUV was packed with as much as it could hold and we left right away, burning up the highway, burning blunts, and listening to 8-Ball and MJG "Lay It Down" on repeat. We had an eighteen-hour drive ahead of us.

We stopped in Chicago and I was mentally and physically drained. I wanted to eat and sleep. My cousin had other plans. He was always the life of the party, so it wasn't surprising when he found a bachelorette party at the hotel we were staying at. We ended up hanging out with the girls throughout the night, drinking and assuring bridesmaids they may one day be a bride. There went my good night's sleep. I woke up the next day in one bed and my cousin was in the other. Girls were everywhere. I had two in my bed and he had three in his. Boy, did it go down that night. We woke up at the same time and started laughing. We went back to sleep then snuck out of the room to go have breakfast and gas up for the remainder of the trip. He told me that was the way to cap off my rookie year, toast to the NFL life.

I got to Minnesota and needed to de-compress from the season. I was happy to be home and have all the comforts I grew up with, seeing old friends and hanging out with family. I started hanging out with a girl I knew from high school named Michelle. She was my first real crush. I liked her a lot and could definitely see us settling down together. She had family from Nebraska and we talked every so often ever since college. We were out one night hanging out at a club and having a good time. Right when I thought I was going to close the deal and take her to my crib (the honeycomb hideout) and do work, she disappeared. I didn't know what happened or where she went. She didn't tell me. I was pretty confused and even more so, when shortly after that, I found out she was married to someone. I wanted so bad to settle down and plant roots but just felt like I was always finding the wrong ones. I felt, if I couldn't trust someone I knew since high school, I probably couldn't trust anyone.

I called my agent to find me a trainer and just ate, slept and lived football. I didn't go out the remainder of the offseason. I felt I was in a good position and the whole situation was for the better as it set me back into football mode, not letting things like girls and partying derail my career. The NFL is the type of business like, "What have you done for me now?" I knew it didn't matter that I played well at the end of the season, it would only matter what I brought back to camp with me. They are always trying to recruit to replace you. You have to take it with a grain of salt, but it can definitely keep you up at night.

The only bad thing about the off-season is being home and too accessible. What I mean is that the more you are available, the more chances there are for people to ask you for money, better yet to expect money from you. I always say that the main people who will destroy you are the ones that are closest to you. That's not an opinion, that's a fact. The reason they can so readily is because they have you emotionally attached, know what makes you tick and have years of things they can use to throw in your face. Needless to say, that fact didn't pass me up. I won't lie and tell you I handled it right, but I will tell you I didn't know how to say NO or to deal with it. Hence why I mentioned in an earlier chapter about the two answers athletes need to know and use.

I couldn't handle the stress and wanted to get back to Buffalo to get away from it all and get my mind ready for the season. I was also starving for female companionship. In reality, I was probably more craving a deeper relationship with my mom.

I was twenty-three and started seeing a girl named Stephanie, whom I had met the previous season. I met her in Toronto when I was at a club. She had an ass like J-Lo and a face like Sade. I definitely had both heads working when I was trying to talk to her. Hell, I was at the club with a model from Africa and was still trying to pull other girls. Again, nature boy style in effect. I didn't fully trust her but really enjoyed being around her. We started building a relationship slowly. I felt I was in a safe place and around safe people to focus on my job and personal life going into my second season. One of the best things I thought was that she didn't know anything about sports or football. I remember after the first time I hit it I didn't call her on purpose for a week or so.

She called and was livid but I gave her the excuse I was working and dropped the NFL thing on the down low. Little did I know that the reason I was convincing myself to go forward would be same reason I shouldn't have.

About to roll out on the Patriots. I knew back then that they were a great team and organization. That always brought out the best in me.

Twelve

WHAT SOPHOMORE SLUMP?

I was ready for training camp. I was at 238 lbs. with five percent body fat, a huge improvement from the prior year. I was more comfortable with the process and got the regular practice shorts at camp this year. I was a better player, physically and mentally. The biggest jump in a player's career usually is in his second or third year. I know a lot depends on other factors, but by that time, you can usually tell if a guy can play or not. This season would be a learning lesson on and off the field, to say the least.

I personally think we still had the "*Music City Miracle*" hangover. The team was mostly the same as the year before, except for the ongoing quarterback controversy between Rob Johnson and Doug Flutie. The weird thing was that Doug Flutie led us with a 10-5 record the year before but was named the back-up heading into the season. Rob was good, but Doug was head and shoulders better. Rob hadn't learned how to lead yet or play in big time games. I think the coaches didn't know what to do because of the love affair the fans had for Doug but they were paying Rob top tier money. If the coaches or the powers that be don't make the right decisions, I fully believe the "football gods" make you pay for it. Heck, Buffalo hasn't been back to the playoffs since.

Heading into this season, I was confident that I belonged but saw that we had two established starters ahead of me. I knew I had to be on special teams. The problem is that we hired a guy named Ronnie Jones who had never coached special teams before. Let alone, we cut a lot of our core special teams guys. We basically sucked on special teams. The silver lining was that I played well on special teams and made some waves in the league. As far as playing defense, I didn't get my chance unless someone got hurt. I got in against the New York Jets and got my feet wet. I was out there just running around like I was in practice. That game was a glance of what was soon to come. Next thing you know, John Holecek (the baddest white-boy I ever played with) gets dinged and I get in for a full quarter against the Kansas City Chiefs on the road. If you don't know, I'll tell you that Kansas City quite possibly had the loudest fans ever. Lucky for us, we won. Winning is the ultimate high, especially when you help the team win. For the next two games, I kept getting in and was doing well. We played the Tampa Bay Bucs the following week where Sam Cowart hurt his ankle after getting a cheap shot block by Frank Middleton.

This was my chance. You hate getting your chance because one of your brothers got injured, but in this business, you have to take it and not look back. The game was going well and I was in for a few plays. I stayed in so much that I started talking shit to their sideline after a big hit. I motioned to Derrick Brooks that I was the real number 55. That was a dumb ass young player wanting to be noticed. Derrick went on to the Hall of fame and even better person after football.

I was dumb, but back then I didn't care who it was that was in front of me, I would try and destroy them. Late in the game, we needed a huge stop and it got to the fourth down. We called a sellout blitz to stop a run play. Their running back was Warrick Dunn, who I used to watch on TV. He was short in stature but ran tough. I assumed he would run into the line and set up a field goal try. He was an all pro and he didn't, he set my ass up because I was fast flowing and cut back on me and in my gap to score a twenty-yard touchdown. Those few plays I made earlier meant nothing, because I felt like I was the sole cause of our loss. That's one of the biggest differences in college and pro games, if one person makes a mistake in the pros the offense will score more times than not.

Calm before the storm! Game face and attitude was always on point!

Once I got into the locker room, I found out that Sam would be out for the rest of the season. After a long week, I made a promise to myself that I had to ball out like never before. I cut entertaining women and drinking. I had four games to show anyone that was watching or listening that I belonged and that they made a mistake in not drafting me. Through those four games, I racked up forty solo tackles, and twenty assisted tackles to end up with sixty overall. My best effort was a twenty tackle game against the Seattle Seahawks to end the season. We ended up 8-8, not making the playoffs and not living up to expectations. Shortly after the season, John Butler, who drafted me, left for the sun of San Diego. Next thing I knew, Wade Phillips was fired.

I was shocked! If the general manager gets fired, every player has a target on their backs to be released. With the firing of Coach Wade, our offseason was going to be short as we would have to come in and do agility testing for the new coach, Greg Williams. He had to make his decisions about which of us he wanted to keep and who he was releasing. The weight staff got fired, the scouts got fired, and even the trainers got fired. The first defensive meeting we had, everyone was on edge. After the practices, we were free to take our offseason break.

My rookie class met at the airport before a few of us flew out. We gave each other hugs and got contact information because we didn't know who was or wasn't getting cut. I wasn't a starter, so I knew I could be replaced. I felt like my time in Buffalo would come down to the draft pick. If they drafted a linebacker in the first three rounds, they were going to put him on the field. I was sitting with my dad watching the draft. Buffalo drafted a kid from Virginia Tech, Corey Moore. I sat quietly for a minute and then decided I needed to figure out the game plan. My agent went to Buffalo and found out they were planning to have Corey in my position and didn't know where they were going to put me.

I was super stressed. I didn't know what this meant for my future. I started playing golf during this time to learn how to decompress from thinking about my future all the time, even during sex! The one thing I picked up was GOLF! The best thing about golf is that it allowed me to play with my dad and spend time with him that I usually wouldn't get. It also allowed me to play with my friends who were in the corporate world so I could learn and LISTEN to what their lives were like.

Regardless, football always came first. I was on a tight workout schedule, but really needed the people that always made me feel better, my boys and my college friends. We would typically take a trip in the offseason, but I invited them all to my house. I told them we could barbecue, play golf and go out. I rented a few limos and flew in friends like, Jerad, in town to celebrate. He was a old roommate from college who actually left Nebraska and went tot another school and did really well. After his stint in pro ball it was always good to see him and other guys from college. I needed their support and friendship during this time. We always had a good time. I had it planned out that we would go to the cigar bar, have drinks and catch up, then go to a club called

South Beach. We were going to stop by the strip club as well. One of my cousins really wanted to tag along. He is a bit of a wild card. He enjoyed the moment too much and sometimes thought that because he was with a bunch of football players, he could act any way he wanted and do anything. Typically, if I talked to him beforehand he would tone it down, but with the number of guys there and the egos, he was jockeying for a position.

He came to the limo with a big gulp drink from 7-Eleven filled with alcohol. That should have been my first warning of the state of mind he was in at the time. He was the type of drinker that would get aggressive. We went to the cigar bar then walked to the strip club. The limos were going to pick us up to go to the club later. I was never a guy who went to a club and looked for trouble. It was always about hanging out with my friends and looking at girls. My cousin, for whatever reason, would go up and talk crazy to the girls. While outside of the strip club, he randomly cussed a girl out that was just walking up the street. We were all talking to him, "What are you doing? You're so disrespectful... just chill out!"

By the time we got to the club, we couldn't get in because the girl's boyfriend was the bouncer and he refused to let any of us in because my cousin cussed his girl out. We were all furious! I told my cousin he was done with us for the night and asked the limo driver to take him home and come back to get us. We were going to hang out at another club nearby until the limo got back. We were trying to make the best of the night. My friend Doug from high school went to talk with this one girl not knowing her boyfriend was there. Her boyfriend got mad and two different times they had to be separated from yelling at each other. This night was going from bad to very bad. I honestly couldn't wait for the limo to get back, especially when I saw a huge group of guys hanging outside with the guy my friend got into a yelling match with. They were waiting for us. This was not what any of us needed. I called the limo driver and couldn't get through. It kept going to voicemail and the club was about to close. The bouncer told us we had to wait outside for our ride. By this time, I had been calling the limo driver for almost three hours. I was mad, tired and now had to sit outside with this group of guys who wanted nothing more than to jump us.

Slowly the group of guys started walking toward us. They had bottles in their hands and had a plan of what they were doing to each of us. By the time the limo finally arrived, we were in a full-blown brawl. We managed to hop in the limo one-by-one and get out of there, but one of the guys hit Jerad with a bottle and shattered his eye. It was horrible. I had the limo driver take us to the hospital as I yelled at him about where he was for the past few hours. As it turned out, my cousin, who was supposed to get dropped off a short distance away, intimidated and threated the limo driver and made him pick up his girlfriend and drive around while they hooked up in the backseat. Now, here we were all bruised up and my former friend and roommates eye shattered, all the while my cousin was intimidating the limo driver. I was so mad.

I was at the hospital and had to call his mom and explain to her what happened. He had to have surgery and stayed in the hospital a little while. I felt so guilty. He only came down because I begged him, and now he was hurt and had life-altering injuries. I realized how easily that could have been me and I would have messed up my career. I was so pissed at my cousin too. He ruined our trip by trying to be a big shot. I had a great offseason until the last two weeks that were so negative.

I had no control over anything and just wanted to get back to Buffalo to get away. Every day, I know I am blessed because I know that could have been me and not Jerad. That night still haunts me to this day. I always wonder what if or what could have happened had the night not started on a bad note.

***The point in this story is that people you hang with or associate with can or will put you or friends in harms way. Be careful of your surroundings and that includes who you hang out with.**

As you might guess, I wanted to get training camp started just so I could get my mind off what transpired back in Minneapolis. Camp was hard both physically and mentally. The first three weeks I wasn't myself, I was thinking way too much and wasn't as focused as I should have been. Somehow and someway I made it through and did enough to still be around. When we broke training camp, it was a release. I beat Corey out for a spot and everyone else they tried to throw in there. I was now motivated and focused to make the best out of this year. I worked out early in the mornings, then ate breakfast and watched film. It helped me play better but also it kept me busy so I couldn't think about my friend who was still hurting.

One morning there was a note from a security guard on my stool. It was a note to call a lady in Minnesota about a situation that arose. I had no idea what it would be in regard to, but was shocked when I got on the phone and there was a motion for a DNA test to determine if a child was mine. Apparently, a girl I had dated in high school many years earlier saw a write up of me in the paper in Minnesota and thought she would go on a hunt for child support. She had a child who was seven or eight at the time and was claiming he was mine. I was more than shocked, I was nauseous and angry and sad all at once. Thoughts flooded my mind from having to pay back child support, to not being involved in that child's life for so many years, to planning for that child's college. I would go from stranger to paternal figure and back to stranger with every second.

I knew this girl had a child years earlier, but there was never any mention of the baby being mine. I was so upset because I was in a new relationship with Stephanie. What if this kid was mine? How will that change my whole life? When I was supposed to be focused on the season, all I could think about was if I had a child out there and didn't even know, on top of what happened in the summer. I went to downtown Buffalo and took a paternity test. It was very weird getting my mouth swabbed. I felt like everyone was looking at me like I was irresponsible. It was embarrassing and frustrating at the same time. I didn't tell Stephanie about it because I thought it would only really matter if the baby were mine. I was already worried, no need to let her worry too.

A few weeks later after a hard practice, I went home and Stephanie had cooked dinner. We were sitting down to eat and watch TV when my phone rang. It was an unknown number and Stephanie was looking at me, it was that look like, "I see this number is unknown and you are hesitating answering it, for your own safety answer it now!!!"

It was the lady from Minnesota about the paternity test. Stephanie could hear it was a woman's voice and was staring me down. I had been so much in football mode, I forgot about the results coming in. I took a deep breath as she said, "As far as the matter of paternity, it is 99% sure you are NOT the father." It was a true Jerry Springer moment as I thanked her and danced around the house before telling Stephanie what happened. It was such an intense and turbulent time for me to realize a simple newspaper write-up on me in the local paper was enough to have scandalous people lie for notoriety or money. I was relieved but didn't want to give any more thought or energy to the situation. In all honesty, I felt bad for the kid, not knowing who his dad was and for his mom who was being a cleat chaser, but it was time to think about myself and the family I was creating with Stephanie.

Time to turn and burn, about to go wreck havoc on a running back.

Thirteen

Out With the Old, In with the New

My third season was the most intense learning experience with a new coach, defense, and general manager. The offseason seemed like it never ended because we had extra meetings and practices due to the league rule that new coaches had extra organized team activities. OTA's were full speed and just as long as training camp. With this being a pivotal year, my agent set some goals for me. I needed six tackles per game on average and a couple sacks and my stats would be with the top outside linebackers in the NFL. I would have taken those stats any year to be honest. It took me a very long time to pick up the forty-six defense Gregg Williams installed. It was so bad at one point I thought I was going to get cut. I was in thick competition for the starting spot and it came down to the last preseason game. We played Pittsburgh and they were known to be a tough physical team. With the right mindset and faith, I ended up having a great game with eight tackles and a tackle for loss. This was the break I needed and earned through hard work to take into the regular season.

Our first game of the season was against New Orleans. We got destroyed. The second game was the week of September 11, 2001. We had a home game that weekend so a few friends came in town for the game. We were playing play station that morning cutting up like usual. We got a phone call asking if we were alright or knew about what had just happened. We turned on the television just as the second plane was going into the tower. I didn't really fully understand the impact of the situation at the time. We all suddenly started thinking who we may know that lived in New York City and what we could do. My friend Matt worked in one of the buildings. I was horrified thinking I just watched his death on television. We called him for days, until we found out that our buddy, who was never late for something a day in his life, missed the bus for the first time that day and wasn't in his office when the planes struck. Watching it live was surreal in the sense I couldn't believe something like that could happen on American soil. The whole day felt like a time lapse with none of us knowing what to think or say.

Most of my friends were stuck in Buffalo and our games were cancelled for a week. We got a few extra days off until the league figured out what we were going to do about the games that weekend. The only good thing was that I had a house full of my closest friends who I truly missed. We finally had practice that week and everything seemed out of sorts. The locker room was usually loud and boisterous, but after that day it was somber and quiet for a long time. It took some time for everyone to get back to our personal realities and not get caught up in the horror of all our country was going through. I think it was felt throughout the NFL in general. Every hold over player wasn't too fond of the new regime that came in, and needless to say, didn't want any additional bad news. Most guys felt the less time around the stadium, the better.

The first year with a new coach absolutely sucked because the team was usually gutted and the wins are scarce. We weren't any different as we ended up at 3-13 for the season. I think the best game we played was when we played the Carolina Panthers in what was named the "shit bowl" because we both had the worst records in the NFL at that time and whoever lost would be considered the worst. When I say we played like it was our last game, multiply that times ten. We won because we were less shitty than they were and they had some young players on their team. I hit or surpassed all my goals my agent set forth and I was excited to see what would happen in the off-season. I will tell you this, when you know you might not get paid, it consumes you until it happens or you find out your fate. I think I checked the internet four times a day to say the least. No news was neither bad or good news.

My agent called me and said my contract was signed for a year at $500,000. I was pleased with that and wanted to come back stronger. I mainly stayed local, looking to get a bigger apartment with Stephanie. While unpacking our apartment, I turned on ESPN and saw that the Bills signed linebacker Eddie Robinson. Apparently, he was close with Coach Williams. I had no idea what this meant for me. I knew they weren't bringing him to the team and not planning to make him a starter. I was pissed off and called my coach and asked him to be straight with me if I was getting cut. I just signed a year lease on a new apartment. He assured me he hadn't heard anything.

I called my agent next and he also hadn't heard anything about me getting cut. He urged me to keep practicing and participating like normal. During practice the next week, Coach Williams walked right up to me, "We signed Eddie Robinson, the Houston Texans needed a starting linebacker, and we need a returner. We traded you, we still love you and you did a great job, but you're not with the Bills anymore." The way he said it made it seem so casual and light even though I felt like I got punched in the gut. I had no choice but to gather my things and go home to tell Stephanie. That's the NFL. Things change in the blink of an eye. I got a call from Houston to leave the next day. I didn't know much about Texas, other than I didn't like anyone from there while playing in Nebraska.

I flew down the following day. I walked outside of the airport to what felt like the hottest place on earth. It was like 100 degrees and 97% humidity. I got picked up and driven straight to practice. They were in full fledge practice the entire offseason. The stadium was being built, so we had meetings at a hotel and practiced in the Astrodome. After my first training session, my dad called. I told him I didn't think I was going to make it, it was too hot and they were working us like slaves. I couldn't make it through a practice without feeling sluggish. I was a bit dramatic but was having a hard time adjusting. I had a former college teammate that was there as well, so that was nice to have a familiar face.

Battle Red Day - Take the head off the snake and the body will follow. Back in this time knocking people out was the culture. These days it means a big fine.

After a couple weeks of practice, I was second team. I knew training camp was going to be hard. I was 235 pounds and needed to get to 245. It was a very difficult camp. Guys would run down and take on the wedge with blocking pads on going full speed. The coaching staff didn't seem to care about our bodies too much. We had to go hard even in practice. There were guys breaking shoulders, getting knocked out and being on injured reserve just from practices. There was so much to get used to, other than the weather and coaching. It made it easier when Stephanie moved down. I felt some type of normalcy. I was in my prime years, but professionally playing for a franchise team who, at the time, didn't put in the best effort to win. It was so hard pulling into the stadium knowing there was a high percentage chance we weren't going to win. It was hard to get motivated. I oftentimes tried to remember what Coach Osborne would say, "It takes a true leader to lead a team into certain death, but still find a way to come out on top and play well." That's what I did. I stayed optimistic and played hard even though there was a good chance we would lose.

One game we didn't lose was against Dallas. We practiced against them in the pre-season. We did well defensively. We played them on a Sunday night. The stadium was electric and it was a great atmosphere. We won and you would have thought we'd won the Super Bowl. The stadium was shaking. The crowd erupted at the end in full pandemonium. It was so loud. Everyone got a game ball that night. That was when I realized football in Texas was different than any other place I know. It was way bigger than a team; it was the way of life. For the next several weeks, I didn't pay for a meal anywhere I went. Everyone and their grandmother's wanted to treat me and any other players like we were their family.

I started to enjoy the area a little more and invited friends down to visit often. Jerad came down one weekend.. Before he came down, I went and bought a brand new Ford Expedition. It had all the bells and whistles. I paid cash. When Jerad came down to celebrate a game with me, I gave him the keys to it. It was a good moment; we both were teary-eyed. He and I never showed much emotion but that day we did.

I didn't give him the care as a charity case but as a token of appreciation for being a brother, friend and supporter. Even though he was going through a difficult situation, he had always been there for me ever since college. He believed in me and had no ulterior motives which was nice to know. I was so happy and proud to do something nice for him. He **deserved** it and I was fortunate to be able to pay it forward for him. One thing I admire about Jerad is that he still went on to make a great life for himself. He became a major Division One strength coach, and now is a director in a tech company in Las vegas. Good things will always happen for Jerad because he's a good man. Even though the friendship has changed I'LL NEVER NOT BE THERE.

*** One thing is true in life. Relationships and people change, that doesn't mean that you have to. Always remember when you do things with the right and good intentions it won't matter what people think because they are most likely projecting a bias created by themselves or someone else.

Perfection! Nothing like a big hit to change the game.

After a year in Houston, I balled out and entered the free agent world. I led the NFL in tackles and ended up with over two hundred for the year. After the season, I changed agents and went with a guy from Minnesota, Mitch Frankel, who my godmother recommended. He was a decent agent, average at best, but I liked his partner Jeff and they had a young intern I liked as well. A great agent is going to get you the best deal every time, regardless of where it is. Mitch wanted to get me the easiest deal so I would just be signed somewhere. It became common knowledge that he would do the best things for him, not his clients. For example, Houston sent out a lame offer, Mitch called me for it and it was totally a waste of time. Why would he even bring that to me? He just wanted to get me somewhere so he didn't have to think about it, that's why. I should have Jerry McGuire'd his ass and made him say "show me the money."

I knew a couple scouts and general managers in different places. I talked to Green Bay and Atlanta myself and had great conversations.

They asked if I would leave Houston, and I told them absolutely. My linebacker coach at Houston called and asked if anyone was calling me, so I told him about my conversations. I was on my way to the airport to go to Green Bay. It was an early morning flight and I had twenty missed calls from the stadium. I texted my agent and he said not to answer, to let them call him. As I was walking on the plane to go to Green Bay, they finalized the deal for me to play in Houston, $12 million for four years.

I was locked in. I could start thinking about my future and starting a family with Stephanie. We got married during that time and life was good. I still had her sign a prenuptial agreement. It wasn't personal, just business. I had financial security and was really excited to help a franchise team develop into a winning program. Houston was a great city, and the fans were amazing. They knew football and were patiently optimistic knowing it would take a little time for us to evolve. I was happy to be a part of it. Little did I realize that building a winning franchise was a lot harder than I ever envisioned.

Me tackling Emmitt Smith in the very first game in Houston Texans history. This was later in his career, but he still had skills to bring it. After we won this game we couldn't do wrong the rest of the year.

Fourteen

HOUSTON, HERE I COME

I was used to being on winning teams from high school to Nebraska and Buffalo, so being part of the Texans during this time had its difficulties. We didn't win much in 2003 or 2004; we never had the chance to be in the hunt. The 2003 season, we ended up 5-11 as injuries destroyed our defense. We were all walking around wounded. In 2004, we were 7-9. We were closer that year to a playoff but couldn't manage to make it happen. We were on a losing streak and went to Green Bay for a Sunday night game. We lost 16-13 and I hurt my shoulder taking out some linemen. I didn't think anything of it at the time, but found it strange the next week when they benched me from the game to give a younger guy some action. That upset me as it made me aware they were unsure of my contribution to the team. The following game against the Jets, I got a cheap shot and tore ligaments in my ankle and cracked my tibia and fibula.

This was the excuse the coaches needed to get me off the field. I had two options - have one surgery and rehab myself back to health or have three surgeries back-to-back to get healthy as fast as I could. Houston wanted me to have the three surgeries telling me they needed me on the field immediately. If they were getting rid of me, I wanted to rehab and not put my body through multiple surgeries. I had my first one, but was having a hard time getting the rehab specialist to call me back to set up rehab appointments.

Before my second surgery, my agent told me that Houston would keep me and we could work on getting healthy, but we needed to go through with the second surgery. My wife was nine months pregnant and scheduled to have our baby the next day. The last thing I wanted to do was go into surgery and be sore and in recovery while my daughter was being born, but I needed to be back on the field for Houston as fast as possible.

My first season in Houston was great for me personally, but we sucked. Good thing about the NFL is that you get to play against some great players. Here I'm sacking Donovan McNabb. He was way before his time in regards to being a dual threat.

I had a strange feeling but decided to go through with it. I decided to do the surgery March 1st, but by the time I was in the operating room, I was put up for trade. I woke up to the realization that I could have just done rehab to get better, but Houston told me they needed me only to trade me once I was out.

Advice for all athletes: GET A SECOND AND THIRD OPINION.

As angry as I was about my career, I needed to switch modes since Stephanie was being induced for our daughter's birth. I went from the surgery room to the labor and delivery room. I woke up starving. I wanted a shower and food. I went home and got something to eat, but within forty-five minutes of me leaving, her water broke. She wasn't progressing how they wanted her to and the umbilical cord managed to get wrapped around my daughter's neck. The doctor rushed over to me and asked how strong my stomach was. I told her I thought I was fine, to which she replied I needed to get changed because we were going to have an emergency cesarean.

I was concerned because it was all happening so fast. I sat in the area by Stephanie's head as I watched the doctor and nurses take my wife's stomach apart. It was so intense. The doctors pulled my daughter out and I kept waiting to hear her scream. I had no idea what was happening, but do remember they seemed to be tossing her around like a loaf of bread. I kept thinking, "Oh my God, they are going to break my baby." She started screaming and it was the best sound ever. It's strange that a cry can be confirmation that everything is alright. The doctors brought our daughter to us to meet her for the first time. It was such an emotional, crazy experience. We were crying and laughing.

That day, March 2, 2005, Soleil Foreman had arrived. She had full eyebrows and looked just like me. It didn't hit me until that very moment that I was a dad. I was scared to death but knew there was nothing I wouldn't do for this little girl. I immediately started thinking of all the wonderful things in life I hoped she would experience, as well as planning for her future. I lived for a different purpose now. I would do anything for this person that I didn't even know yet. It was by far the most life-changing experience and one of the greatest days of my life.

I had so much love coming out of me for her. I was bawling, which was probably a bit alarming to Stephanie since I was not known to show too many emotions. It's amazing how a child could cause such an affect. My dad used to tell me if anyone ever messed with me, he would kill them. I thought he was a bit dramatic, but now I totally understood. My biggest concern was how to take care of my wife and child. I was motivated yet still had the itch, I wanted to play football again.

I seemed to bounce around for the next two years. They always say, "There is a thin line between starting on a team and being on the couch." The Giants called me to do a workout. I did well and ended up signing with them for the last half of their season. I got Lawrence Taylor's locker. It was awkward, as I would be changing to see a huge picture of Lawrence Taylor looking at me. His locker was right by the door. The greatest part of it is that LT wrote a book and I read it in two days. The story that stuck with me was that he used to sometimes have women before the game. I can remember being a dumb-ass rookie and thinking, "Let me try this, if LT can do it, so can I… maybe it'll be a good luck charm." To this day, I laugh about it. LT was on one of those morning talk shows my grandma used to watch and I remember her calling and telling me about it. Little did she know her grandson was trying to emulate LT, but in the wrong way. It didn't affect my game, but it became a good luck charm my first year or so. Thank God for airline miles.

The media in New York was intense and would just walk right into the locker room regardless if we were clothed or not. Female and male reporters were all up in our grill. After a while, I just got used to it. They didn't care that I was butt naked doing an interview.

I loved being in New York. They had a first class organization. The player liaison was amazing. He would talk to me about life after football and tell me about various internships available. He set up massages at my house. There were several small things like that, but the big picture makes the player's lives much easier.

The coaching staff and players were all very respectable. They treated me like I was with the team from the beginning. The little things mean so much to older players in the league. Most teams don't get it because they are too worried about spending an extra thirty-grand on an employee or benefits. We all know most teams waste that on the over-blown budgets they give the higher ups. There is a reason why certain teams and organizations are always on the hunt and others aren't.

Tom Coughlin ran a pretty tight ship. If a meeting started at 8:00 AM, you were late if you weren't there at 7:50. I learned that one time when I thought I was early and the meeting was already in progress. He always wanted us to get that extra ten minutes of tape or knowledge. He was by far the best NFL head coach I got to play for. He was an intense "win at all cost" type of coach.

We played Oakland to win the division. It was raining hard, but before the game, Coach Coughlin said, "I don't care if your mom's out there and a monsoon is coming, we have a job to win the division and win at all cost." I like that style of coaching. If he's all in, I'm all in. That was a guy I could play for. He was very inspirational and welcoming. I always felt like a bit of an outsider since I came on late. I remember after one game, I kept saying, "You guys did great." He would correct me and say, "WE did great!" He was just an outstanding coach to be able to learn from. We lost that year to Carolina to finish our season. Coach Coughlin thanked me for my efforts.

I never played a full season again. I was a middle season sign for people on injured reserve. I played the following year in San Francisco. It was during that game that a rookie decided to close his eyes to tackle someone, landing on my MCL and tearing it. I remember lying on the field waiting for the training staff to get to me, looking at the lights and thinking that was it, when my career would end.

The game and the players were changing. So many were on HGH or steroids. I knew in order to compete I would have to do the same and didn't want to. My time went quickly, but it was time to hang up my cleats on my NFL career. My neck and back were shot and I was scared to run into a pile like I used to. Becoming paralyzed was a possible outcome. That's another thing I remember from LT's book. He knew when it was time to stop. For me, it was time.

If you're not ready to run through a wall on game day in the NFL, you have no soul.

Fifteen

The Beginning of the "End"

It was New Year's Eve 2007 and Stephanie came out to San Francisco to help me through rehab and get me home. I had a brace on my knee for my MCL tear I suffered in the game in Seattle. Funny thing is that the brace went from my ankle all the way up to my hip. Normally an MCL injury isn't viewed as serious but mine was a grade three tear. When it happened, that injury hurt like hell and burned like my skin and knee were on fire. Needless to say, I was happy to see someone besides the training staff.

After going out on the town, Stephanie and I went back to the hotel early to spend time together. We had a great night together ringing in the new year, if you know what I mean. Next thing you know baby number two was on the way. With another child on the way and a destroyed neck and back, my perspective in thinking about hanging up the cleats became clearer. The NFL can be a harsh reality of how quickly things can change in the world of sports. No matter how well most guys think they are prepared, they certainly aren't.

For the next few months I flew back and forth from San Francisco to Charlotte for rehab and to check in with the doctors. This was a time of serious thought, contemplating whether or not I wanted to play again.

Just in case I changed my mind about going back into the game, I attacked rehab as if I would return. I spoke with my agent about twice a week and one thing I didn't want to go through was being a "camp body." A "camp body" is a guy they sign that they know they most likely won't keep and bring in just for camp or someone they bring in just to push or develop into a young guy/player that needs to get his shit together. As the months passed, my decision became clear to me that it was time to let go of the sport that had taught me so much in such a short time. On to bigger and better things was my mindset.

The time came for our daughter to be born, and we had a scheduled cesarean. This time, it was much easier as it was planned. It felt like an oil change appointment. I thought I would hold it together better since I already had another daughter and knew what to expect, but all the emotions came back when we met our youngest, Ciel Foreman, on September 17th, 2007. She was perfect. Ciel looked just like me and it hit me deep that I had two beautiful girls that I had to provide for and protect until I kicked the bucket. After getting everyone home and settled, I decided to fax in my retirement papers to the NFL. It felt weird faxing in what felt like a death certificate to an unknown person but in reality every player is just a piece of meat that will eventually expire.

Later that month, I went to Minnesota for my dad's ceremony going into the ring of honor for the Vikings. In my opinion, it was something long overdue but I was happy for him to get some of the just due that he deserved. It was a surreal moment, watching my dad give his speech during halftime of a game having just faxed in my retirement papers seventy-two hours prior. I didn't tell my dad before his ceremony because I wanted to keep all the attention from our family and media on him.

From my perspective, it has always felt like politics and bullshit has kept my dad out of the Hall of Fame. I do know for fact that there was or is people not wanting him to get in, which to me is flat out stupid. I believe God will eventually get him in, I just pray it's when he is still alive.

During my visit for his ceremony, we were able to have some "father-son time." I was now an adult we could talk about real life stuff and anything else that came to mind. During our talk my dad asked me, "How do you think your marriage is going to be after football?" I was a little surprised he asked that because I didn't expect anything to be different and felt Stephanie and I were stronger than ever after having our second child. He told me that things are always different after the NFL and some people or couples make it but most don't. That hit home, because as I thought back to when I first moved to Minnesota after dad retired, I do remember times of my dad being sad or upset. I suddenly realized what he went through was what I was soon to face but in a different way. I didn't give it much thought at that time but things started to change soon after we got home from that trip.

I won't go into details, but like most marriages that end, it takes two to tango and two to leave. One thing I believe affects most marriages with athletes is that they have notoriety and the wives have a very hard time transitioning out of the league because they have as much identity with the NFL as the player himself. That is odd to me, because not one time have they practiced or played a game. When you are playing, the going is good, but when you retire, or better yet, when the NFL retires you, things change rapidly.

Tips for a professional athlete divorce:

1. Always have an attorney on payroll. Most good attorneys have seen and dealt with any situation you will face. They can provide a perspective that you will need in order to protect yourself.
2. Find a counselor or pastor who you trust and feel comfortable enough to talk to. As men, we generally are scared to express ourselves, but trust me, during these times you need someone to discuss things with. Family is good but you never know where they stand until the dust clears.
3. If you had a prenuptial agreement between you and your spouse, stick to it. You spent money and time for it so stick to it.

4. Understand that your personal business is just that, YOUR PERSONAL BUSINESS. Protect yourself and your business with a mindset that the more people know the more they can hurt you. I had a guy who I played with in Buffalo and who actually lived by me in Charlotte go behind my back and feed my ex my thoughts and such. Funny part is that homeboy was a fraud and was on the creep the whole time. The same people you may be confiding in are the same ones who could be stabbing you in the back.

5. Understand that you haven't failed but you are in the process of learning more about yourself and others around you.

6. Hire someone to double check your finances and your financial advisor. Most of the advisors are living off what you make and aren't looking out for you as their client. Truth be told, Jon Kubler stole almost $200K from me. The worst part is, I thought I could trust him because I had known him since college.

7. Man up!! This means to face any mistakes you made, or was made against you, with the same intensity and vulnerability you would before and after a game. It takes a true champion to stand up for himself and/or face any mistakes he has made.

Sixteen

Dark Days

With my personal life starting to change rapidly, financial downturn, and the growing number of family and so called friends working their hardest to send me to the poor house for their gain, I realized that I was all alone. What I mean is that in the city of Charlotte I had nobody I could trust. The messed up part is when I would call people who I thought would be there to just listen, but they didn't want to hear my problems and seemed to just not care.

The feeling of being alone, scared, and deserted can and will drive you crazy. It sure did me. I remember the times when I would be thinking to myself about different things that I might have missed in the past or other situations and would look over at the clock and BOOM two hours had passed. Divorce is never easy and will always be a mental challenge and drain. If you don't have a few true soldiers in your corner, you are as good as dead! I was fortunate to have my mom, Jamal and Samer. The latter two I've known for over twenty-five years. In many ways, Samer and Jamal are more like family than some of the ones who share the same bloodlines.

Regardless of what was going on inside my head, I knew I had to look into finding a way to bring home the bacon. Looking for a job or career at that point in time was tough. When I got in front of someone to talk about work, the main thing I would always hear was, "Wow, you played football, so why are you looking for a job?" Crazy how the common person thinks every player is set for life, but the reality is, 99% of guys have to find another career after retirement.

One thing I knew I would do well in was anything to do with football. At the moment, it dawned on me to try my hat in the sport I hated, I went through my cell phone. Plenty of names were there, but not much opportunity except for one. Frank Solich said he had a position for me in the weight room and I would help out with the team also. My first reaction was that was a shitty job but the smarter side knew it could lead to something better either there at Ohio State University or somewhere else. There was one big roadblock. For some odd reason, I was informed the rest of the family wasn't going to come along. Amazing the difference, because had I been cut or traded I don't think it would have mattered!!

After seeking a job in coaching and turning down Coach Solich, I decided to look for a career back in Minnesota. After about three months, I had a couple things lined up with the help of Jamal and my dad. When it comes to knowing people, my dad is an ace in the hole and he did a lot of the legwork. He always said to me "I may not have a whole bunch of money but I know a whole bunch of good and important people." After flying up and interviewing with two insurance companies, I decided on the one with the most potential and upside. I chose that company because they had some Nebraska ties. One thing you can count on from people in Nebraska is that they are loyal and honest (except Jon Kubler).

After agreeing to take the job, I flew back to Charlotte to face the harsh reality of life without a family. Most importantly, it was the life I never wanted for my kids - a split family. I lived it as a kid, and definitely didn't want to re-live it as an adult. I'm an admitted control freak and not being able to control this situation was a hard pill to swallow. Now onto one of the days I'll never forget.........

I rented a U-Haul and packed a few things from my house. I didn't want my kids to come home to an empty house so I decided to take the things I needed and leave the rest. After all, I was never one for material things. The hardest part was that my oldest daughter, Soleil, was having a preschool play that day. I sat videotaping her with tears in my eyes because I realized how much both my daughters' lives were going to change when I left the next day. I felt all the feelings I had as a child without both my parents being together. I didn't want that for them, but knew it was out of my control. Fighting back the tears, I went to the restroom to compose myself. I could feel my heart pounding so hard that I thought I was going to have a heart attack because I was out of control and crying so hard. I finally pulled myself together and put on a brave face for Soleil. I still have some of those pictures from that day and I look at them from time to time just to keep things in perspective. It reminds me of how far I have come as a parent and a man.

The following day, I gave my girls the biggest hugs and kisses after dropping them off at school as I got in the U-Haul and drove fifteen hours straight to Minnesota. I was overcome with grief and emotion. I balled my eyes out the entire ride out of North Carolina. One thing I will always remember was that I had no regard for my life during that trip and decided to drive straight though ice storms going seventy-plus miles per hour. I really didn't care because I was so wired that I didn't want to sleep and I knew my mind wouldn't shut off.

I talked to my mom on the phone non-stop, sobbing for my daughters, yelling about my life and wondering how I got to that point so soon after football. As she talked to me my entire drive, she prayed over me and spoke blessings into my life while telling me it would be

"O.K.". When people tell you that it will be "O.K." you never truly believe them because most of the time the person telling you is just giving you lip service. But my mom was different because she had been through it herself.

Seventeen

Who Am I?

I arrived in Minnesota in one piece by the grace of God and began the process of wrapping my head around my new life. I moved back into my bachelor pad that my dad had lived in ever since my second year in the league. From NFL star to living at home with my dad, what a life. With things changing so much it was hard not to think about the past because it was so new. Thinking about the past was the worst thing to do. The best thing to do is to take it day by day and keep stacking good days together. That might seem trivial but it's a big deal.

That first year was extremely difficult because I fell into a deep depression and shut down from everyone except my kids. I felt inside that they were the only ones I could trust because they were so pure. I did seek out a counselor. I had hoped a therapist would help me feel better about myself and my situation but that didn't work because all I ever heard from family was that I needed to chill out and that I was crazy. I would think, "Well, how the f*** you want me to act?" It seemed easy for them to say because it wasn't their financial freedom or kids on the line.

Very soon, I began to revert back to what I had stayed away from in other times of crisis - booze and women. Most of the time they go hand in hand, but even when I wasn't out with women I was drinking heavily. Sometimes I would go buy a forty ounce and drink it while driving around Eden Prairie (where I'm from) just so my dad wouldn't see me or ask why I was drinking. I'd walk in, shower and go to bed hammered. Even with a new job, drinking and sleeping around with women, I always kept the focus on when I would fly to see my daughters. One thing that saved me was that I had a few buddy passes that allowed me to fly back and forth for pretty cheap.

There was one weekend that I went to Charlotte to visit the girls that I will never ever forget. It was Memorial Day weekend and I planned some fun things for the three of us to do together. It wasn't until I landed in Charlotte that I realized my direct deposit didn't go through and wouldn't hit my account until the following week due to the holiday weekend. I didn't have enough money for the trip, but I was still able to get a rental car. I didn't have enough money for a hotel the first couple of nights. I couldn't believe this was my life.

I decided I would pick the girls up in the morning and bring them home in the evening and sleep in my car. It seems drastic but where else would I sleep? It was during those lonely nights in my car I felt my absolute lowest. I couldn't afford a hotel, a warm shower or anything. It was the middle of summer, but I was shivering in my car trying to sleep with my clothes rolled up for a pillow. I would drive to the local YMCA and sneak in to take a shower the following morning before going to pick the girls back up. *One thing sleeping and living out of your car for 6 months will teach is who is and who isn't in your corner. As I look back I think it's funny how during that time I could never get a call back or a reply to a text. I can remember times when all I wanted was to "vent" and then I'd hear dial tone shortly. Needless to say those same people were the ones who were trying to be at every game etc... I think the worst/best story is when I had a sibling post on her social media that she was happy my ex got* her "NFL" money. LOL, *I was aware of alimony etc but "NFL" money talk from a sibling was lowdown and low class(blood/last name doesn't make you family). Finally, at the time I hated it and myself but it was one of the beter things that I have went through in my life.*

I felt so embarrassed and horrible about doing it and that really hit home when my kids would ask "Daddy, why can't we stay in your hotel and have fun?" Man, that hurt and still does. I told myself that was the moment I would never forget and I would never be there again. I was never going to let anyone or anything put me in this position again. As horrible as I felt then, I am glad now it happened because I now know it was one of those learning experiences my mom always preached about.

My mom was my rock during this time. She knew how I was feeling and did all she could to help me, and then some. She called and checked on me every day, motivating me to be a better person for my girls. One conversation we had was about the turn around. My mother talked to me like never before and challenged my manhood. She would say "I didn't give birth to no pussy and I'll be damned if you will let a divorce send you to your grave." I swear she said that to me a thousand times. If you know my mom, then you know she won't hesitate to repeat herself. To this day I can hear her voice coming through my phone as it seemed my ear was suction cupped to the phone.

Slowly, I started getting healthy. I quit drinking and started working out. I had to learn how to value myself. I had to successfully transition to being a single dad and an everyday guy that I liked. I felt less pressure and focus on me and more focus on the positive things, like work and kids. It seems so easy to say, but I swear, it was like moving earth at that time. No matter how much progress I made, I knew I had another hurdle to conquer and it was well overdue.

With a long divorce, shady financial guy, missing cash (that has never turned up) and creditors calling me about loans that had been opened in my name, I had no choice but to file for bankruptcy. You wonder how I got into a place of bankruptcy? Easy answer - I trusted the wrong people and was too eager to please those who were never grateful. I didn't end up broke but damn close by my standards. I actually held off on filing bankruptcy for almost a year because of pride and what people associate it with. They look at you like you're a criminal, which isn't the case. I'd bet a lot of bankruptcies come from divorce. Hell, the lawyers will send you to the poor house faster than your ex's. Like I said before, that pride pill is hard to swallow. I eventually saw it as a way to not be held accountable for others' doings and to get my life back in order. One thing I thought about was when my kids turned eighteen, I wanted be able to help as much as I could with college. If I continued to wait that would mean it would take that much longer to get my credit back into shape.

I knew the way to come out of that situation was to be structured. I would make lists of things I needed to do daily to better myself. I came up with this plan because I remembered back to what made me perform better at football. When I was playing, I liked to have daily, weekly and seasonal goals. I felt the structure of goal setting and working to reach those goals was part of the reason I felt I could overcome any fear I had on the field. I thought why not try and make everything into football terms and see how it goes.

Later that year, my daughters came to visit for two weeks for Thanksgiving break. I was truly the happiest I had been in such a long time just enjoying life with them. I was truly thankful to God for giving me two of the most beautiful girls. We had an amazing time sledding in the snow, taking them to the Mall of America and best of all, just daddy/daughter time. The worst part was the night before they were to fly back to Charlotte, I found myself in my room crying as I packed them up. I knew they needed me in their lives more often, and in all honesty, I needed them as well. I realized these girls were my motivation for living. They were what I needed to make myself better. The proudest moment was when they heard me crying and walked into my room and covered me in hugs and said, "Daddy, it will be ok." They were empathetic to the situation even as young girls. They didn't understand but knew I was hurting, and sweetly wrapped their arms around me, rubbing my back. I can't describe the emotion I felt, but I knew I would do anything for them and, if that meant strive to be healthy and successful so one day we could have the type of relationship my mom and I have now, I would do it.

Eighteen

A New Life and Refined Man

After finally focusing on working hard and making the most out of my situation, I began to see a bigger picture. For almost eighteen months, I drove back and forth from Minnesota to Nebraska every week just so I could have some structure in how my weeks would all be the same. I would leave early Monday mornings and drive back Thursday nights. That's one of the advantages of a sales job, freedom. The best thing that came out of all those miles was the "shield time" I had to think about things deeper, smarter and on a broader scale. It actually cleared my head more than I realized at the time, and it let me see and view people in my life the right way. After about fifty-thousand miles on the road, I was given the opportunity to move to Nebraska with the same company. Initially, I didn't think it would be a good move because I had been gone from Nebraska so long and I always thought, "What the f*** was going on in Nebraska?" Little did I know that the move to Nebraska would be just as big of a decision as when I chose Nebraska to attend college. You could say, this time Nebraska chose me to show what a great place it could be.

As a side note, after my divorce, I ran through plenty of women from models, old flames, socialites and new flings.   At the time, I thought it was what I was supposed to do, and boy did I do it well. I was like a savage beast but in a good way. I conquered plenty, but loved none.

Speaking of love, little did I know that moving to Nebraska would not only be the best thing for me mentally, spiritually and personally, but it would help me love again. By love again, I mean more than just a female. I began to love myself, life and oddly enough, I started to love football again. Moving back to Nebraska forced me to think about football because everyone in this state eats, sleeps and drinks Husker football. In order to not sound stupid or negative, I mainly watched games so, when approached, I knew what I was talking about. The majority of Husker fans are pretty damn smart football wise, not the case in other places. The other crazy part is that even with having been an introvert my whole life, I started being a frequent guest on T.V. and radio stations in Lincoln and Omaha. If you knew me while I was in college there is no way you'd think I'd be in front of any camera, let alone voicing my opinion about the Huskers.

Over time, I felt comfortable to trust women again and actually started dating. That didn't go too well for a couple of reasons. One of the biggest reasons was me, I still had a major wall up and really lost all empathy when things got emotional. I think a divorce changes you to be more matter of fact and to focus on the facts. The other reason was that majority of the women that were around my age had been run through by a host of former Huskers. I don't judge, but I never was one to cross dicks with a teammate unknowingly over a female. The kicker to that point is that there are a lot of former Huskers that are either "haters" or "captain save a hoe." The latter was an epidemic amongst my former brethren. I could go on and on or drop names but that's not my style. I think guys in general should take the oath "thou shalt not save," or "bros before hoes." I think if that was something they took serious then I think the world would be a better place.

After being in Nebraska for almost a year, I met a great person through work who would become my best friend, then my girlfriend, and now my wife. Our first encounter wasn't out of the movies at all. She was working in a sister company in the HR department and needed my driver's license. I was managing and selling so I didn't have much time to go to the office. I heard she was a handful but never thought I'd meet her. Next thing I knew, she was calling me non-stop about my license and leaving voice-mails. I finally answered and she tried to rip my ass for not calling back and even threatened to delay my pay. As you can guess, I waltzed right up into her office. As mad as I was to be there, she hit me with her big green eyes and it took me back and the rest is history. We had similar situations with children and former relationships. She helped me see the female perspective as I helped her with the male point of view. We connected on a deeper level as a love formed between the two of us. For the longest time, we denied it and even forced ourselves to date other people. We always knew we had love for one another. I didn't feel comfortable with people knowing at work because they talked too much. Also, with me being single, black and a Husker it seemed like every time I took a shit, a company email was forming. Haters come in all shapes, sizes and colors.

After about four years of working for one company, I decided to leave for another. Normally, this would have thrown me for a loop, but I knew it was for the right reason and would also lead to bigger things between Allison and I. This was our time to really be out in the open and, needless to say, our lives moved at a rapid pace. I immediately called her father and brother up to meet for lunch and to let them know I was going to date their daughter and take care of her the best I could. I don't get scared or worried about any man, but my father-in-law has a little bit of crazy in him that lets you know he'll mess you up if you mess with his daughter.

After two years, we are now married with a blended family of two boys and two girls. After my first marriage, I would have never thought I'd have a son, let alone two. I love kids and I don't care that they aren't my blood, it's all the same. I will say, love has no sight and that's awesome.

**Me and Allison, amazing how a mutual circumstance
can bring two people and families together.**

With all that has happened in my life, I am most proud to be still standing here today. Not a new man, but a refined one and one that needs constant help that I'm not afraid to ask for.   I have daily battles with my back, knees, and neck, but I keep going for my family. Just as I had plenty to play for then, I have plenty to live for now, and that's the only reason I have never given up and never will.

While much of my life from childhood through adulthood I felt I always had to work to reach my goals, I always knew it was a part of my learning experience. I rose to the occasion again and again to succeed with hard work and perseverance. I made it to the top, dropped to the bottom and am now working my way back, constantly making sure I never forgot my grandfather's words, ***"Don't go knock at the door, kick it in and let them know you're in the building."***

Appendix A

Special People:

To the people who inspired me at various times in my journey:

Ken and Phyllis Knapp - You two are like my second set of parents. You guys have made my life great and with all the support you have given me, I can't thank you enough. I still can't figure out why you guys have blessed me by being with me in my journey, but all I can think of is that you two are great people. I thank you for pushing me, telling me when I'm wrong and being supportive when you didn't have to. Ken, I won't hold it against you that you are an Ohio State fan.

Jamal Lewis - I want to say thanks for always being there for your boy and never wanting anything from me. I will say, I view us like brothers. You and your family took me in when I was new to your school and that made my transition easier. I'll never forget that. We've known each other our whole lives practically, and there hasn't been a time you let me down. I respect your opinion and honesty. You always keep it real with me and get me to think about bigger and better. My main man "Reggie."

Jerad - I love you like a brother and will always be there for you as you have been for me. Once we hooked up in college, you taught me a lot about life and exposed me to things I would have never been exposed to. Like we say, you taught me the ins-and-outs and outs-and-ins. You taught me perseverance and I admired you on how you handled things in college when you weren't getting a fair shake. You are genuine friend and I trust you with it all.

Rest of the wolf pack (Sam, Gates and Shawn) - I put you two together because you all were at times my main weekly support system. We have all been down with each other since we could walk and chew gum and we are always going to be down for one another. Through all our rough times we were always there to pick each other up. That's true family.

Papi - What can I say but you were my hero. I hate that you never got to see me play. I used to always want to make you proud. I admire your sacrifice for your family and it's something that has helped me throughout my life. I respected your stern, hard ways. I hate that diabetes took you from me, but I now try to honor you by helping others. I have taken your advice, sometimes too far, and still haven't taken any shit. Love you Papi!

Nanny - You are the rock of the Foreman family. The way you cared for Papi during his last years was nothing short of amazing. The love you gave me when I was younger is hard for anyone else to live up to. What you've done to set the tone for the Foreman's will never be forgotten. The love you have for me and my children is something special.

Justin - As much as it was my time to shine, it's yours now. I find myself happier for your success than mine. Mine wasn't easy, but I feel the time we had on the phone when you were in medical school was priceless. I see in you what I wish I could be. Thoughtful, smart, and thorough comes to mind. What you accomplished won't dawn on you until you get to my age. You are a great father and man and don't ever change. Always protect yourself and your kids first no matter what.

**Me and Justin, he's doing big things in this world and helping
a lot of people. I hope my knowledge and mentoring will
help him stay out of some of the situations I was in.**

Meyer Family - I want to thank you for giving me an opportunity to try something I didn't know I could. You guys stuck by me when I first struggled and kept pushing me to do bigger and better things. You never held me back from bettering myself or other opportunities. For that, I will have the utmost respect for you.

Allison - You are more to me than my wife and partner. We have come a long way in a short time and been through some shit too. Every time, you have answered the bell for me and us. I never had that before and I love you for it. You took me when I was at my lowest and built me up into something that I always wanted to be. You have replaced any assumptions I had about a woman so I could trust again. It takes a special person and woman to deal with what comes with being a part of my life. You have adapted and grown along the way. The way you have loved my kids is something very special to me. You are a great woman and person and I am proud to call you my wife. In life, I always wanted to marry my best friend and you are definitely that. Our bond will never be broken.

Uncle Larry - You are an inspiration to me. I always admired the fact that you went to Morgan State and balled out. You showed me through your actions how to be a head of a household. I still think about when you gave me that talk before I played Ricky Williams. I still hear it, "Jay, you gotta stick his ass, cause he going to bring it."

Uncle Grease - You are gone too soon. You were often misunderstood, but I knew where you were coming from. The advice you gave me before you passed came in handy and I'll never forget it. You made my day when you'd come and record my games in middle school. Your commentary will always be legendary.

Craig - You are like an older brother to me. We don't talk all the time but I always got your back. You're a great father and you taught me that it's ok to be emotional about your kids. There has never been a time I called and you haven't been there. And you I will always be there as well.

Tom Osborne - One of the greatest coaches of all time, but easily one of the best people I have ever met. My early memories are from you as the Husker coach who I laughed at because I was a Miami Hurricane fan and long-time family University of Miami ran through my blood. Once I met you, I felt at home and protected. You provided me with things my dad couldn't. Some lessons I learned by just watching you I'll never forget. I'm truly grateful for you coming into my life. I still remember when you said my position was up for grabs after starting the whole season and going into bowl preparation. Your quote was, "Jay, I don't think you will ever be a burner," I never forgot. You challenged me in the papers and you knew I'd step my game up and I did and started ever since.

Joe-From a spit ball to life long friends. Your unwavering support is hard to find or come by. The tough talks and the messages that I didn't like or want to hear are never forgotten. You are a special soldier!!

Reggie Herring - As the linebacker coach for me in Houston, one of the best coaches I ever had, you never pulled any punches. You challenged me like no other, motivated me like no other and supported me like no other. With that Reggie, I am grateful. You are a true coach in the sense you had a great affect on me in and out of football

My Coaches –Mike Grant, Tony Samuel, Dan Young and Charlie McBride - All of you at one point in time went to bat for me and believed in me. I never knew when, but I knew it, and I thank you for it. All of you at one point in time showed me a way to be successful and then pushed me to be even better. Those lessons I still hold close because I know without one of you I may have never made it.

Mom - You are my rock and without you, I would not be here today. When I ever had doubts as a youngster about if you loved or missed me, you would always send something without me knowing. As an adult, you saved me from suicide and a dark, dark place in my life. When nobody thought I could make it, you pushed me until I could stand up. You taught me how to be a man and to do things I didn't want to for the betterment of my kids. You have filled the missing piece of my childhood and heart that I yearned for. I now know patience and compassion more than ever before. You have always told me when I'm wrong and held me to the fire and for that I can never repay you.

Jason Peter - You are a good dude. You are one of the most intense and loyal human beings walking the face of the earth. In today's world that is hard to come by. That loyalty is and never will be forgotten.

Uncle Butch - You are like a second father to me. You have taught me patience in how you deal with me and our family. The strength you gave me mentally has grown and I love you for it. Everything you've done for me in my life is never forgotten. Your ability to hang tough in tough times is what I admire the most about you. I'll never forget you telling me I was a warrior, even if I didn't believe it, you did.

Dad - Man, we did it. Not always easy or right, but we did it. Even though we had our issues, it will not change that I love you dearly. I saw you make sacrifices in order to make ends meet and provide for me the best you could. I know we were both learning as we went along. You taught me to do anything and everything I can for my kids and that lesson I owe you for life and will never forget. You being at every game gave me confidence to go even farther. I hope I've made you proud throughout life because I am proud of you. I wouldn't change anything but I will say you were right about some things and people. You always look out for me and I hope I can do the same for you.

Three generations of hard heads. Old school all the way to the new.

Soleil and Ciel - You two are my life and my energy. When you two blessed me it changed me for the better. Every day, I think of how I can make things great for you. I miss you dearly but I also know that our bond is unbreakable. Your dad may not know all there is to know about girls, but one thing I will never do is let you down or not try and figure it out. I will be here through every step and will enjoy knowing you are enjoying life better than I did. Always remember that you can always come home to Daddy. Always be there for one another and try your best to make your own way. A dollar earned is better than a dollar given or taken.

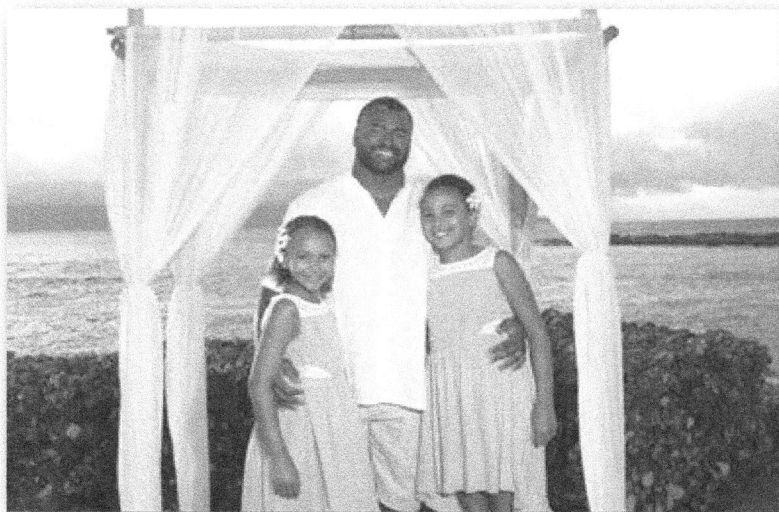

Me and my girls (Ciel and Soleil) on the day I married Allison. These two don't know how they have saved my life. I work hard and pray that every day I make them proud.

Appendix B

Experiences:

As I think back on life, I have had some unique experiences that most kids or adults don't get to experience. They may have even given me a leg up in a way, but if I didn't take them all in, they would have been all for nothing.

- I was a ball boy for two years for the Minnesota Vikings. At an early age, I got to see how professional football players acted and also forged some long-term relationships.
- I was a ball boy when John Randle was an undrafted rookie. I remember calling my dad and saying, "There is this crazy ass defensive tackle from some small school in Texas that is really good but he's a little small." I remember watching him put weights in his pants during weigh-ins.
- Chris Carter took my ass to school on the hoop court and actually blocked my shot so hard he tore all the ligaments in my thumb. I remember how much it hurt, but I couldn't let any of the players know because I didn't want to look like a chump. To this day I haven't gotten it fixed.
- I got to meet Dick Vitale at a Minnesota Gopher game long before he became the icon he is today. I remember him being a nice man.

- I was fortunate enough to get to ride in a limo with John Elway, Bubby Brister, Jim Kelly, Dan Marino, and my dad. Needless to say, I was on cloud nine. Funny thing is that when we played in our first National Championship when I was at Nebraska, we snuck out on New Year's Eve and wanted to get into a club. It was packed and they said they weren't letting anyone else in. Luckily for me and my boys, Dan Marino was walking in. I quickly mentioned my dad's name to him and he got us in.
- Over the years I have been fortunate enough to meet three presidents - George W. Bush, George H. Bush, and Bill Clinton. It's crazy to meet the men who essentially ran the free world. All nice guys.
- Alongside my dad, I have met numerous Hall of Famers. That by itself is an experience people would pay for. Listening to the stories of how they got into the NFL or some of the ways they had to play is truly amazing. That alone always helped me think about the older players rather than the guys that were playing currently.

Appendix C

A letter to my younger self:

Dear younger Jay,

What I am about to tell you is the fool proof way to navigate your young life and career. As you will experience, there will be plenty of ups and downs. Knowing that now, just remember that it's all about how you handle it. The best thing you can do is worry about what YOU can control. There are plenty of things that go on in life and football and you will never know the real reason for the outcome. It's not fair but it's life.

You will experience at least one personal trial and one financial trial. This has been true throughout most people's lives. Football players are no different. Expect the worst and plan for it. A man with a plan is always well off in this world. Use the same fire and stubbornness in your personal life as you do on the field. Be the best you that you can be.

Always be present in your work!!! Would you not attend meetings before a game? No, so why would you not have your finger on everything you do within your life. If you run your business efficiently, then you should run your personal life like that as well.

Don't be afraid to step on toes or make hard decisions. Why? Because the closest people to you will be the ones who will let you down and hurt you. That sounds harsh but that's reality. They know what makes you tick, they know your emotions and they have history with you. They have a playbook on you. Never forget.

Lastly, let your eyes do the learning for you. Peoples' actions are what tell the true story not their mouths. People these days know exactly what they think you want to hear but don't follow through on it. Actions, actions and actions!!!

Here's your checklist:

1. Don't trust anyone. You have a short span to make a life for yourself and whoever you support.
2. You are the ruler. Don't be afraid to be the ruler. This way it's on YOUR terms and not on anyone else's. You give this up and you expose yourself to long-term harm.
3. Have an attorney on retainer. This may sound trivial but let me tell you something, having one will keep you out of a lot of shit. Most attorneys have seen a lot in the courtroom and your life is no different.
4. If you get married, have a serious prenuptial agreement. This for YOUR protection. After all, you are the one who lifted, ran and sacrificed to get where you are. This goes for high net worth people as well, men or women. Make sure you have any custody and child support already figured out because most of the time the opposition will try and pawn the kids and use them as leverage.
5. Don't be afraid to not be married. The life you will live is a hard one and it's not for everyone. A player's wife has a hard role but she has to be OK with playing that role forever. The majority of women don't like that role after you are done playing. If 82% of

NFL players are divorced within two years after retiring, why get married in the first place? It sounds bad, but having children and not marriage isn't a bad idea. Here's why, if you are part of that 82% you will be a single dad anyway. Why pay for another person's exit from the marriage? Look up the origin of the word marriage.

6. Make every decision for the betterment of you and your brand or purpose. Who you are is who you will sell when you are done. Without proper decision making, you might miss out on an opportunity of a lifetime.

7. Play the game. There is always politics, so play the game like they are trying to play you. Playing the game doesn't mean you need to sell your soul, but it means you need to do the right thing in order to get ahead. What's your purpose in life? Go and get it.

8. Don't let pride make you look like a fool. Deacon Jones told me, "That pride pill is a big pill, but if you drink enough water it will go down better." That means, if you have to swallow your pride in order to get another one to three years in the league, then do it. As long as the check clears on Monday, what's the difference?

9. Be seen more than anyone else. When it comes down to nut cutting time it helps to be present. Being present can also lead to getting your first crack at a promotion in the business world.

10. Surround yourself with positive people. When have you ever seen a negative person that is successful?

11. Learn to sacrifice. Sacrifice early for long-term gains. Don't be shortsighted; most shortsighted people are greedy. Greed hardly wins.

12. Most importantly, DO NOT let family or in-laws live with you or overstay their welcome. Not that you don't love or like them, but as much as they are around they could be scheming on your ass.

13. Don't tell everyone all your business or thoughts. This way you won't have to worry about what your enemies know. That means the people closest to you are sometimes the ones that are your actual enemies.

** If you get fifty-percent of that right you will be doing a lot better than most. Always embrace the struggle because nothing great comes from things being easy.

The much wiser and smarter, Jay Foreman

Appendix D

My biggest regret:

I prided myself on living a life without regrets. I figured if I went about life doing everything I could to the maximum and with good intentions, that I could live without ever looking back. It's funny when people say "I told you so." That usually comes after they either watched you make a mistake or found a reason to not be upfront with you. My kids are my life and give me purpose and will be for the rest of my life.

My only regret is that they didn't get to see me play. I wish they had the opportunity to experience me in the NFL, if only for a season. Soleil was very young when my career was ending, and Ciel wasn't conceived until the year I was retiring. Like most parents, I think they deserve the world and that's the part of my world I wasn't able to give them. Obviously, I wouldn't change anything about the timing of their arrival, but if I had one wish that would be it, for them to experience watching their daddy play in the NFL.

Appendix E

The Grind:

I often hear kids and parents assuming that all we did was show up on Sunday and play football in the NFL. I can't blame them because the everyday life and grind to just play a game isn't something that can be glorified, or something that would even begin to seem appealing.

Here is a typical "work" week for me. I did this diligently, week in and week out, year in and year out in order to answer the call and be in my place every week.

Monday: Usually the day after the game and was mostly film and a light lift.

7 am	Wake up
8 am	Breakfast
9 am	Post-Game Radio Show
10 am	Lifting and light running at the stadium
11 am – 1 pm	Film breakdown and game evaluations
2 pm	Another lift that focused on flexibility and endurance in the muscles.
3 pm	Light pre-dinner meal
4-9 pm	Family time
9-11pm	Early start on studying next week's opponent and/or clean up from prior week's game.

Tuesday: League mandated "day off".

7 am	Wake up
8 am	Breakfast
9-11 am	Hard lift on the lower body. I liked hitting legs hard twice a week for stability and strength. I always felt that a stronger lower body lowered the possibility of injuries and fatigue.
12 pm	Lunch
1pm	Chiropractor
2-4 pm	Massage
5 pm	Nerve massage -This one hurt the most but was the most beneficial for me since I had serious nerve damage.
6 pm	Dinner
7-9 pm	Catch up on TV, bills and family time.
9-10 pm	Film study

• • •

Wednesday/Thursday: These two days are the "ball buster', hardest and longest days of the week. We install the game plan and add new plays we think will work against the opponent.

5:30 am	Wake up
6 am	Steam and sauna at the stadium for forty minutes.
7 am	Breakfast
8 am	Team meeting
9 am	Special teams
9:30 – 11 am	Defensive meeting and position meetings
11 am – 12:20 pm	Lunch and lift

12:30 – 1:30 pm	Pre-practice meeting and walk thru
2 – 4 pm	Practice (usually both in full pads but one for sure)
4:30 pm	Post-practice meeting and film review
5 – 6:30 pm	Lift
7 pm	Dinner
7:30 – 8:30 pm	Deep tissue massage
8:30 – 9:30 pm	Studying film

Friday: Usually just touch up and a shorter day.

5:30 am	Wake up
6 am	Breakfast at stadium and early lift
8:30 am	Team meeting and special teams meeting
9:30 – 11 am	Defensive and position meetings
12 – 1:30 pm	Practice (this practice there weren't any coaches "coaching". They wanted to simulate a game for us)
2 pm	Acupuncture
4 pm	Light massage
6 pm until ?	This is when the hay is in the barn and you can go out with your family or position group.

•   •   •

Saturday: Travel day if it's an away game.

9 am	Quick team and position meeting
10 am	Walk thru in all phases
1130 - ?	Off until it's time to head to the airport
1 pm	Flight

5 pm	Usually around the time you're settled into the hotel
6 pm	Dinner
7-9 pm	Meetings
10 pm	Curfew

• • •

Sunday: Game day with noon kickoff.

7 am	Wakeup
8 am	Breakfast
9 am	Church service
9:30 – 10 am	Buses leave for the stadium
12 pm	Kick off and kick ass on the field
6 pm	Usually back home and thinking about the next game.

• • •

Professional sports isn't for everyone, no matter how big or fast the athlete is. It is in the preparation where games are won or lost. I hope this snapshot is a good look into what it takes to make it in the NFL for one week.

Appendix F

The Blessing and the Curse

I get asked all the time, "Would you do it again?" The answer to that question is always, "NO". Regardless of the fame, money, women, experiences, and relationships, I still stand by my answer. I will never shy away from loving football, but I also realize what the game that I love so much has cost me.

On one hand, football taught me more about myself in a short time than I could have ever imagined. I learned how to communicate, deal with adversity, hard work, and set goals – all of which one cannot place a dollar value on and I will forever be grateful for. I never played for the money, but I admit that it was great getting paid to play a sport I loved and it has helped my family and kids' futures. Some could say football has done more good than bad for me and others, and I agree. But……

On the flip side, the pain I deal with EVERY DAY is a reminder of the brutality of the game. The time it takes me to get up and going at such a young age is terrifying sometimes. This is a result of years of smashing my body into men much larger than me the majority of the time. The headaches from numerous concussions and hits has taken over my daily routine and mindset. The mental anguish of knowing your body is broken down and continuing to break down is sometimes hard to deal with. The loss of my mental capacity isn't something I will ever get back, nor do I or will I have the ability to function like a regular forty- one year old. The things that are going on internally are things that nobody can see or fix.

When I referenced the good that one couldn't put a dollar value on, I can double down and say it with even more conviction that what I lost directly or indirectly from the game is more than I gained. The loss of family and friends, some I've known since I can remember, is something you never can plan for when entering or leaving the NFL. What I mean by loss is that you lose people along the way whom you thought were with you for the better, but turned out to be the main people who took advantage of you or purposely screwed you over. I will always wonder, "What if I never made it?" The answer I will never know. I ask myself out loud, "How much are family relationships worth?"

I don't blame football or the actions of others, nor do I hold football accountable, but I do recognize that indirectly through football, there are things that I lost that I can never replace or replenish. Yes, I can forgive, but forgiveness will never replenish what was taken away.

Appendix G

More Photos:

The Foreman side - Soleil, my dad, uncle Butch, me, Ciel and Nanny.

The Lewis side of the family - Me, Soleil, Chandra, Aunt Audrey, Aunt Helen, Grandma Dear, Ciel and O.V.

My dad and little brother Anthony.

First and only game playing back in Buffalo against the
Bills. Revenge was sweet but on the play Travis Henry
got injured. Aaron Glenn on the tackle as well.

One of the most moving days I have ever experienced. I played a
round of golf with some true heroes from the armed forces. Oddly,
we had a lot in common when it came to aches and pains.

Me, Tony Womack, Junior Spivey and Bobby Bonilla. Bobby Bonilla was one of my favorite athletes growing up.

About the Author

J ay Foreman is a former NFL player who played college football for the University of Nebraska Cornhuskers and played in the National Football League for the Buffalo Bills, Houston Texans, New York Giants, and San Francisco 49ers.

In college, Jay was an All-Big 12 Conference Selection for Nebraska. A four-year letter winner, he served as a starting linebacker during the 1995 and 1997 National Championship seasons. He ranks 14th on the Huskers' all-time tackles chart with 233 tackles and was the team captain his senior year. In 1998, Foreman was a semi-finalist for the Dick Butkus award.

During his eight year NFL career, Foreman made two postseason appearances and played for the Houston Texans during their first three seasons as a franchise. Jay was named one of the Texan's team captains and held the title for three years. He achieved five consecutive seasons of over one hundred tackles, two of which he recorded over two hundred tackles with a grand total of 937 in his career.

While playing football at the University of Nebraska, Jay earned a BS degree in Business Administration. During his NFL off-seasons, he completed an MBA program at Harvard University. During his time in Houston, he started a charitable foundation known as "Foreman Friends," an organization that assisted abused and underprivileged kids in group-homes.

Today, Jay continues his work with non-profit groups and various charities. He returned to his college football roots and now resides in Nebraska. Jay established the Foreman Foundation in 2013 and works to raise awareness and enhance the lives of people in need in his community. He and his foundation are focused on causes like diabetes prevention and autism awareness, both of which have a direct personal impact on Jay. Additionally, each year he organizes a turkey drive to help families in need during the holidays by raising funds to purchase turkeys for hundreds of families in Lincoln.

While continuing to impact those in his community through his involvement with various charities, he is also focused on his family. Jay is married to Allison and collectively they have 4 children. Jay has two daughters, Soleil and Ciel. Allison has two sons, Logan and Grant.

www.ingramcontent.com/pod-product-compliance
Lightning Source LLC
Chambersburg PA
CBHW071754090426
42737CB00012B/1811